WHAT'S BUGGIN' YOU?

WHAT'S BUGGIN' YOU?

MICHAEL BOHDAN'S GUIDE TO HOME PEST CONTROL

SANTA
MONICA
PRESS

IN MEMORY OF WARREN HIGHMAN,

WHO BELIEVED IN ME, WAS MY MENTOR,

AND A VERY DEAR FRIEND.

The author and publisher would like to thank Alex Pearlstein for his assistance in writing the manuscript.

Published by:
SANTA MONICA PRESS LLC   www.santamonicapress.com
P.O. Box 1076   smpress@pacificnet.net
Santa Monica, CA 90406-1076   1-800-784-9553

Printed in the United States

Before using any pesticide, pest control substance, or pest control device, readers should always read the manufacturer's instructions and precautions. Should readers have any questions regarding any procedure or material mentioned in this book, the publisher and author strongly recommend consulting a professional pest control operator or public health service official. The publisher and author are not liable or responsible to any person or group with respect to any loss, illness or injury caused or alleged to be caused from the use of any of the products, procedures or information found in this book.

Library of Congress Cataloging-in-Publication Data
Bohdan, Michael, 1947-
    What's buggin' you? : Michael Bohdan's guide to home pest control.
p. cm.
    ISBN: 1-891661-01-9
    1. Household pests—Control.   I. Title.
TX325.B64   1998
648' .7—dc21   98-5210
                                                              CIP

10 9 8 7 6 5 4 3 2 1

Book and cover design by Mauna Eichner and Lee Fukui
Cover photo of Michael Bohdan by Gary Barnes
Pest drawings courtesy USDA, Advanstar Communications and Rick Baker

CONTENTS

ENCYCLOPEDIA LISTING

INTRODUCTION

I nsects have been around for millions of years, and have demonstrated time and again an incredible ability to survive and thrive in great numbers. As a professional exterminator, I can't say I'm altogether upset about this fact. After all, my livelihood depends on the reproductive powers of house and garden bugs. But I'm guessing you could care less about the sex lives of tiny pests, and are more interested in how you can rid yourself of undesirable critters invading your house and yard.

Which led me to this book. In my business, the one question people ask me more than any other is, "What kind of bug is this?" Well, this book will help you identify the pests you're trying to control, and also whether you even need to "control" them in the first place. After all, many bugs are actually beneficial.

Once you determine that your multi-legged invader is an enemy, you need to know whether he's the general, a lieutenant, or just a simple foot soldier. To most people, a roach is a roach, but there's a big difference in the way you control a German roach and an American roach. A lot of time and money is wasted each year on improper treatment techniques.

In this book, I'll teach you my tricks of the trade, tell you a little bit about myself and my industry, and give you some tips and insights on the safest and most effective ways to control pests. Hopefully, we'll have some fun, too!

CHAPTER 1

THE WORLD'S MOST FAMOUS EXTERMINATOR

I was always a curious kid. One time, snooping around outside in Illinois where I grew up, I found some mosquito larvae in a pool of water and thought I had happened onto something great—something amazing. Even though my father later told me my discovery was not as earth-shattering as I had thought, I was nevertheless hooked.

In my neighborhood, I was always the kid on the block who would take you up to my room to show you my "cool" bug collection. Somehow, I just never thought that I should be upset or disturbed by these creatures I was capturing and pinning to boards for show. Little did I know at the time, this hobby would one day lead to a full-fledged career.

I majored in zoology in college. I knew that I wanted to work in nature, with the earth's creatures, I just didn't know specifically how I'd make money at it. After school, I found a job as a sanitarian, inspecting restaurants for insect infestation. That gig eventually led to a stint managing restaurants in the Chicago area.

But as anyone who's lived in Chicago knows, there comes a time when you reach your limit of winters. You look up at the flocks of birds migrating south and think, "Man, I'm jealous." My wife and I decided the time had come to leave Illinois and we followed the aroma of barbecue down to Dallas, Texas.

After some serious soul searching, I decided to try to make a living doing what I loved to do so much as a kid: I started hunting bugs again. Back then, some 20 years ago, you just had to pass an exam to gain accreditation as a pest control specialist. Nowadays, with all of the different kinds of chemicals in the industry, it's a little tougher to break in. Not only do you have to apprentice for a year, but it's also necessary to continually update your base of knowledge. I go to continuing education classes to this day.

But I digress. Let's talk some more about bugs. As I gained experience in the industry, I realized my job would be loads easier if my clients could tell me more about their pest problem than just, "Michael, it's big and black, with a whole heap o' legs." So I started putting together a portable display of various insects that my customers could use to identify the critter causing them so much trouble.

I'd take the collection to garden clubs, homeowner associations, client's homes—basically any place where people had a pest to identify. Seeing people's reactions to the collection got me to thinking about the relationship of mankind and insect-kind. I realized that if people got more involved with bugs—even had some fun with them—it not only made my job easier, but also gave me a great way to teach folks more about these creatures with which I'd always been fascinated.

Along those lines, I eventually hit upon the idea of holding a contest to find the largest cockroach in Texas. Bug hunters are a lot like fishermen; every roach they've ever caught grows to be "yay big" with each new telling. Their hands spread wider and wider until they claim to have seen a cockroach the size of a mid-size Chevy. It was time to cut bait or fish.

Well, the contest was a lot of fun and a big success. Somehow, the people at *The Tonight Show* got wind of it and asked me to come out to Hollywood to appear with Johnny Carson on national television. For a humble Dallas exterminator, this was big news, let me tell you.

Michael Bohdan on the Johnny Carson Show

Ed McMahon, Johnny's long-time sidekick, had told me before the show that my appearance would change my life forever. Boy, was he ever right. The actual time I spent on the couch next to Johnny was just a blur. I've since seen tapes of my appearance and can barely remember even being up there.

But Ed was right. The show did change my life. Combat, the insecticide company, had seen my appearance and wanted me to go around the country and host competitions to find the area's largest cockroach. Soon, this premise got old and needed to be spiced up a little. So the contests became a showcase to find the most creatively dressed cockroach in town. The first prize of $1,000 ensured that we'd have at least a few entrants, but I was

Over 75% of the people who entered the
World's Largest Roach contest were women.

happily surprised at the enormous crowds these events would
draw.

At Parrot Jungle in Florida, the turnout was especially huge.
Just about every town we'd go to would make a big fuss over the
contest and we'd have roach after roach presented to us for judg-
ing. And here's a fact that might surprise you: over 75% of the
entrants were women. So you can toss that stereotype of the
screaming lady hopping up on a chair to escape a spider right out
the window!

If you're wondering whether roaches are hard to manipulate
into costumes and dioramas, they're actually quite easy to handle.
When they're dead, of course. Dried up, their exoskeletons pre-
serve quite well. Because of this, I'd save one or two of the "best
dressed" roaches at each competition for a little collection I was
accumulating back home. I didn't know exactly what I'd do with
them, but it seemed like a shame to waste such great handiwork.

When the Combat contests finally ended, I had a brainstorm
about how to use all the roaches I had saved from the various

events. I thought, why not open up a cockroach museum? I sort of had a feeling there wouldn't be much competition out there.

And that's what I did. Here in Plano, where I live, I converted some of my office space into the Cockroach Hall of Fame. In addition to the costumed roaches, I display other species of bugs, informational exhibits and even some prehistoric insects suspended in amber that I picked up in South America. Upwards of 3,000 people visit the museum every year, and many of them leave with a T-shirt. Nothing gets a conversation started like wearing your Cockroach Hall of Fame T-shirt out on your first date. The Cockroach Hall of Fame was even featured in the book *Offbeat Museums*.

Even though there's a lot of fun stuff in the museum, I also include some useful information to give visitors a better understanding and appreciation of insects in general. It all goes back to what I realized a long time ago when I first started my business in Dallas: If you make bugs fun, people will learn.

Of course, I'd be lying if I said the costumed roaches weren't the highlight of the museum. We even have a few bugs based on

The Cockroach Hall of Fame is located in Plano, Texas

Photo courtesy Cockroach Hall of Fame Museum

famous people. There's Liberoachy, dressed in sequins and playing the piano; Elvis Roachley, Marilyn Monroach, and, of course, H. Ross Peroach, done during the 1992 presidential campaign.

Marilyn Monroach   *The Statue of Roacherty*

One of the favorite "non-famous" roaches is the "Don't Drink and Fly" display, which features a drunk roach crashing into a telephone pole. There's also the bride and groom roach on top of the wedding cake; the "killed in Combat" roach resting peacefully in a beautifully crafted coffin; and beach roach, dressed in sunglasses, drinking beer and surfing. Even though the costumes and displays are all in fun, I'm still amazed at some of the time and effort people put in to get the intricate details and outfits just right.

I'm basically a one-man band at the museum. I run my pest control business from 5 AM to 1 PM, then head to my store, The Pest Shop, and museum for the rest of the day. It's a lot of work, but I wouldn't have it any other way.

Despite the long hours and rigors of the business, I still like to get out and be in the public eye once in a while. There's probably a lot of the showman in me, and I enjoy talking about insects on television or radio, maybe even springing a hissing roach on an unsuspecting talk show host now and then.

After *The Tonight Show*, I was lucky enough to appear on *Hour Magazine* with Gary Collins, *P.M. Magazine*, *Live with Regis and Kathie Lee*, *The Joan Rivers Show*, *To Tell the Truth*, *Good Morning Texas*, and many others. CNN covered my first outdoor cockroach race in New York, and ABC, CBS, NBC, the *New York Times* and *The Wall Street Journal* were among the 40 news organizations that covered my first Roach Olympics, held at the Philadelphia Zoo.

Even the Smithsonian Institute in Washington, DC, asked me to help them put together an exhibit on cockroaches. At the party celebrating the completion of the exhibit, guests were offered tasty little cockroach-shaped candies. I thought that was a nice touch.

In addition to the media work, I also accept many speaking engagements at industry conventions and gatherings. On these occasions, I usually haul out my trusty speech — "The Cockroach Approach to Public Relations" — and give the audience advice and tips on drawing more attention to their industry and themselves.

As you can see, I've come a long way from spotting mosquito larvae in a pond in Chicago. Heck, I may just be the world's most famous exterminator.

CHAPTER 2

PESTS AND MAN

When people say that insects have been around before we were here on Earth, and will survive long after we've gone, they're probably right. Few of nature's creatures are as adaptable and hearty as the bug. In the pest control business, just when we come up with an effective treatment for a particular insect, they develop a resistance to it and we have to start over from scratch. People often say that because the cockroach has been around for 350 million years, we ought to be able to learn something from him. But I'm not sure how much we can learn from a creature whose favorite things to eat are dog food, beer and bananas!

Estimates vary on the different kinds of insects that currently "crawl" the Earth. Guesses range anywhere from 750,000 to over a million and a half species. The total number of insects alive at any given moment is impossible to even estimate. But scientists have tried to make analogies like "the total weight of bugs is greater than the total weight of any other species, including mankind" blah, blah, blah. All you need to know is, they're clever, tough and breed like the dickens. Insects make rabbits look like cloistered nuns.

There are five times as many insects as all other types of animals combined.

The females of some species lay up to a million eggs in their lifetimes, with these eggs often hatching long after mom was crushed under the weight of someone's foot. So for everyone who has a notion that we'll "defeat" the insect world some day, get real. It ain't gonna happen. We as humans have to respect the fact that our development is displacing insects and other animals from their natural habitats. Also, it's time we realize that not all insects are harmful or destructive.

Insects basically suffer from the same problem that afflicts the Hunchback of Notre Dame, the Phantom of the Opera, and other freakish folks. Because they're ugly, we assume they're dangerous and should be feared. But just as Quasimodo had a good heart, and the Phantom was one heck of a kisser, many "ugly" insects help us in ways you'd never dream.

Take the beetle for instance. When one of those suckers scurries in front of us on a garden path, it's all we can do to stop ourselves from treating the little guy to a tennis shoe sandwich. In reality, that beetle is serving as a valuable food source for useful animals like birds and lizards. It's also preying on even smaller insects like aphids that damage plants and destroy gardens.

Anyone who's read *Charlotte's Web* knows that spiders are actually big softies. And anyone who's seen a web full of flying pests knows that spiders are like nature's flypaper, capturing any bug foolish enough to cruise into their "cobweb condo."

I think part of our problem is that we're afraid of things that go buzz in the night. The fact that this legion of little critters is scurrying around when we're sleeping or not paying attention really freaks us out. Psychobabblers have come up with a fancy word for a fear of insects—"entomophobia"—but I prefer "bug-brained." Bug-brained people stomp on every spider they see, crunch every beetle and molest every moth. They fill their homes with so many bug-bomb fumes they end up risking their own health more than the insects'.

Now, I don't want you to think that I'm against insecticides, or the proper control of household and outdoor pests. But I think people would benefit from a little more common sense and self-control when they encounter an insect on their property. The other day, I had a woman who was originally from New York call me out because she found one cricket in her house. I told her that just because you see one cricket doesn't mean there are ten thousand of them hiding behind your closet door waiting to jump you. Not every insect is a cockroach.

Scientists discover between seven thousand and ten thousand new kinds of insects each year. They estimate that nearly ten million more are yet to be discovered.

Part of the problem may be movies like *Arachnophobia* that put the idea into people's minds that spiders can take over your house and drive everyone crazy. Why do we need spiders for this when in-laws already do such a bang-up job? Seriously, though, the odds that anyone would ever be driven from their home or apartment by an insect invasion are probably 1,000,000 to 1.

You'd have a better chance of seeing the Cubs win the World Series in your lifetime.

All I'm trying to say is we shouldn't throw out the baby with the bathwater. There are techniques and treatments we can use to control our pest problems without resorting to overkill.

We're never going to come out on top in a war against bugs, but we can still win a few battles. The key is knowing when to raise the white flag, and put down the Black Flag.

CHAPTER 3

INTEGRATED PEST MANAGEMENT

It may sound a little highfalutin coming from a pest extermina-tor like me, but the term "Integrated Pest Management" (IPM) nonetheless refers to a more holistic way of controlling insects than the old method of spray first, ask questions later. It has proven to be quite effective since its inception a number of years ago. Originally a strategy developed to help farmers, IPM soon drew notice from the pest control industry, eager to find less toxic techniques to control pests. Basically, IPM uses technical infor-mation, a watchful eye on the pest population and other tech-niques to control household pests.

Insecticides are one prong in the IPM attack, but we try to keep their use to a minimum. Rather than blast a bug with a bar-rage of spray, we have gradually learned to get a little more creative. Excessive use of pesticides sometimes leads to a concentration of chemicals close to where we eat, work, sleep, and play.

If properly applied, the four basic steps of the IPM system will decrease the frequency with which pesticides are used to control insects. The four steps are:

1. **Identify the pest problem.** Just because you see one bug, it doesn't mean you have an infestation. Don't overreact. Try to determine if a problem exists and how to treat it.

   For example, if you find a few ants chompin' on the Twinkie you left on the kitchen counter, figure out if they're the relatively harmless crazy ant, or the more dangerous imported fire ant. It's crucial to know if the pest is worthy of all your worry.

2. **Know its biology.** Understanding the life cycle of a pest will help you manage it. If you know mosquitoes breed in water, for instance, you can control them by eliminating or controlling sources of standing water.

3. **Know the "action threshold."** A few ants on your counter is not a good enough reason to haul out a host of chemicals. Rather, determine if the population of the offending insect is large enough to constitute an infestation. Does it adversely affect your "comfort zone?"

   Action thresholds vary, depending on the pest and environmental conditions like weather and humidity. Taking excessive or uncalled-for action against a pest can lead to such environmental problems as groundwater pollution.

4. **Use the most effective and safest pest-management plan.** If you can banish the critter without using pesticides, all the better. If you do have to use sprays, make sure you use them in moderation and with the proper supervision and background information. The approach of a few decades ago to "nuke" any bug that you see is no longer acceptable. We should not be afraid of chemicals, but

they need to be used properly. Without chemicals, the bugs would have taken over the world a long time ago.

Nowadays, there are a whole heap of non-chemical treatments for insect infestation that you may also want to try. For example, introducing a benign predator insect to devour the unwanted pest is an option. Also, a simple herb or food product is sometimes enough to drive a bug away. We'll get into this in more detail later in the book.

In the garden, IPM strategy is broader. Besides identifying the problem, and establishing action thresholds, you'll want to closely monitor your garden and decide if short-term, or longer-term controls are necessary. See chapter 5 for more information.

Bottom line, IPM is a good way to keep your home pest-free and an equally successful method for controlling insect problems should they "crop" up.

At 13 inches, the tropical stick is the longest insect on record. Interestingly, however, it cannot fly. The length of fairy flies (wasps that parasitize the eggs of insects) is microscopic—measuring less than one-thousandth of an inch.

🎬🎬🎬🎬 Movie Review 🎬🎬🎬🎬

Skeeter (1993)—A new monstrous species of mosquito bred on toxic waste invades the desert town of Mesquite and sucks some serious blood. I have to say, I liked this movie. The acting was actually pretty good, and the crow-sized mosquitoes they made for the film were fairly lifelike. I did have one or two questions, though, like: How could the larvae and pupae survive in the toxic waste when every species of mosquito needs a very specific type of gestation liquid to survive? Also, I got the sense that some male skeeters were doin' some blood-sucking, when everyone knows it's only the adult females that feed on blood. Other than these minor details, however, I enjoyed the flick a lot.

(All reviews are on a scale of 1 to 5 roaches, with 5 being best.)

CHAPTER 4

PREVENTATIVE AND LOW-IMPACT TREATMENTS

One of the basic principles of IPM strategy is that if there's a non-chemical, low-impact way to resolve your pest problem, try it before you haul out the industrial strength stuff. Look at it this way: If you've got the proverbial "guest who won't leave" parked on your couch, isn't it easier, safer and more prudent to take away his bowl of chips than aim a shotgun at his head?

Now, most of us in the extermination business are not anti-insecticide, per se, we're just going about things a little differently these days. The emphasis is on finding alternatives to the old "nuke 'em" approach. IPM takes more time, patience, and money, and demands that we learn to accept bugs as an unavoidable part of life. It also lets us in the industry, and you at home, control pests more safely and efficiently in the long run.

Sometimes, the best weapon against a meddlesome insect is a rolled-up newspaper or particularly hard-soled Hush Puppy. Back in prehistoric times, I'm sure they beat bugs to a milky pulp with clubs and stones. Nowadays, we clip on a handle, perforate the end and call it a fly swatter. Whatever floats your boat is fine with me, as long as you don't endanger yourself, your loved ones, or your keepsakes when you run around the house like an lunatic trying to kill one little mosquito.

In this chapter, I'll give you an overview of preventative and low-impact treatments. We'll start with treatments which are effective both indoors and outdoors, before moving onto treatments meant specifically for your home, and closing with those aimed at protecting your garden. Remember that this chapter is simply meant to introduce you to some of the wide variety of treatments that are available. For specific ways to get rid of your house or garden pests, consult the Encyclopedia in chapter eight.

Diatomaceous Earth

Before I get into preventative and low-impact treatments meant specifically for either your home or garden, I'd like to briefly talk about DE, which can be used in both settings. When it come to pest control, the initials DE do not stand for Douse Everything. They stand for Diatomaceous Earth. Say those words 10 times in a row really fast and you'll realize why we use the initials.

In its natural state, DE is a soft, rock-like compound that looks like snowflakes, but actually consists of the skeletons of tiny freshwater or saltwater creatures known as diatoms. Before it is commercially sold, DE is mined from the earth and is crushed to a fine dust. This dust feels smooth to the human touch, but to an insect it has very sharp edges. When put on a household pests,

DE is able to cut the exoskeletons of the insects and absorb the waxy coating that covers them, creating a laceration of the exposed tissue. Death by dehydration occurs to the insects within a few hours. Since insects are the only creatures covered with a waxy coating, no other organism—including humans—is at risk for this rather unpleasant demise. In addition, because DE contains over a dozen minerals, it is actually beneficial to soil, which in turn makes for healthier plants.

In fact, DE's uses go beyond controlling pest infestations. In the pool industry, for instance, DE is used for pool filters. These other DE formulations are completely different than the formulation used for pest control—the sharp edges are rounded off through a heating process—so make sure that you purchase the correct product if you are going to use DE as a low-impact treatment.

DE treatment is effective on a number of pests including ants, cockroaches, and silverfish. The only potential problem for humans is breathing too much of the stuff, which isn't recommended with *any* kind of dust.

Indoor Treatments

By taking the necessary steps to seal off all insect entry points, you can ensure that bugs won't have a way into your home. At the very least, even if they find a way inside, they'll have nothing to sustain them.

Similarly, controlling your home's temperature and eliminating dampness will go a long way towards making your house an unpleasant place for bugs to vacation. Doors and windows are ideal places to start. Not only do they let in cold and moisture, but improperly sealed points of entry will prove too tempting for insects to ignore. When one of 'em sounds the bugle that there's a breach in your defense perimeter, it's not long before the whole bug battalion musters for the invasion.

Use common sense. If a window breaks, fix it. If a hole tears in your screen door, repair it. If a guy in a homemade mosquito costume keeps holding your front door open, kick him in the shins!

Constructing a Home

Obviously, if you're starting from scratch, it makes sense to take preventative measures from the get-go. During home construction, wood should not have any direct contact with the soil. Most homes are constructed with pine (cedar, cypress, redwood, and oak probably offer the best resistance to termites), and when a termite gets inside the walls of your home, he can't tell the difference between a wood stud or a fallen pine tree. Pre-treatment of the wood studs with a product called Borates is one way to keep these pests at bay. Course sand or sandblasting sand ("00 Grit") is another method to consider as termites have a hard time penetrating this size of sand. Use either of these methods behind the walls where plumbing is located, in crawl spaces, under the foundation, at all bath traps, and around the outside foundation of the home. Since most pests come from the outside, using boric acid dust on all outside walls during the construction is a good idea.

Wood fences are particularly prone to termite attack because they are in direct contact with the soil. Use metal posts and make sure the pickets do not touch the ground. Defective roofing, as well as an uncapped chimney, can also provide handy entry points for the enterprising insect. Finally, cracks in your foundation are a great way for bugs to sneak into your pantry, so regularly check your foundation for damage.

Protect Your Pantry!

Many pantry pests thrive in a humid environment, with temperatures between 75 and 85 degrees Fahrenheit. Ventilating your cupboards keeps the humidity down. It's also important to regularly wipe or vacuum cupboard shelves. If you can keep crumbs off exposed surfaces and out of those little nooks and crannies at the back of your pantry, bugs looking for a cheap buffet will be forced to go elsewhere.

Opened packages of old food products are probably the biggest source of pantry bug infestations. A box of cereal with one insect could be teeming with them a few weeks later. All food stored on cupboard shelves should be in containers with tight-fitting lids. The reproductive cycle of some insects can be less than three weeks in hot weather, so check packaged items weekly during the summer and monthly in the winter, and remember to rotate all grain-type products.

It is a good idea to know what you're looking at, so take a moment to familiarize yourself with the pests that may be making themselves at home in your pantry.

Beetles like to feed on prepared cereals, biscuit mixes, herbs and spices, dried fruits, and flour. Weevils prefer rice, unmilled wheat, and dried beans and peas. Mites will eat just about any-thing—even wine and rotting potatoes. Cheese skippers, not surprisingly, like cheese, as well as fish and cured meats. While moths don't consume food products, their larvae are fond of dried fruits, nuts, cornmeal, and other grains (it's usually the kids that eat you out of house and home anyway).

If you find even one insect, or tiny punctures that indicate probable pest penetration, the food should be placed in a plastic bag and tightly sealed. Then go ahead and toss the bag in the outside garbage. Any foods near an infestation area should be put into clear plastic bags for several days so you can closely inspect them for insect life.

Infestations typically occur after packages of food have been opened and stored for a long period of time. So it's a good idea to buy only what you will use in a few months. In general, keeping a lot of excess food laying around is just asking for trouble.

As far as the kitchen as a whole is concerned, watch for cracks in the walls, ceiling or floor where insects can lay or hide their eggs. And as gross as it may be, pull out your refrigerator and stove once in a while to sweep out the gunk, junk, crud and spuds that have fallen back there. There's nothing a bug likes more than a dimly lit, romantic meal under a major appliance.

Also make sure to clean all counter and tabletops regularly, and wipe up spills before they become watering holes for thirsty critters. When you throw a perishable food item into the garbage, always put it in a sealed plastic bag, newspaper, aluminum foil, or anything that will help mask its odor and keep insects away.

In terms of plumbing, keep all sink and disposal drains clear, insulate your cold-water pipes and make sure the point where the pipe and wall meet is well sealed and airtight.

Now, I don't mean to scare you here, but I will. Even if you make sure all the food in your kitchen is sealed off from bugs, you still may not be bug-free. A lot of things around the house are edible for bugs, although it's not obvious just by looking at them. The list includes: Spices, Christmas dough ornaments, "popcorn" packaging material, medications, stuffed animals—even table centerpieces made with dried flowers and seed pods are part of a bug's balanced diet. So, if you can, inspect these items regu-

There are more species of insects than any other sort of organism in the world.

larly for signs of insect life. You—and your teddy bear—will be glad you did.

Storage Spaces

You know those expensive quilts, afghans, and high-quality fabrics you've got stored securely in your broom closet? If you don't check them occasionally for insect infestation, these heirlooms will never be passed down from generation to generation because nobody will want the half-eaten things.

A dark, unused attic is another favorite place for cloth-eaters to congregate, making it a dangerous place to store valuable fabrics. And as long as you're up in the attic checking your stored material for insect life, take a quick look at the wall and ceiling joints, as well as the floorboards of finished-off storage rooms. If there are cracks, insects could easily come inside, and if the wood is rotten, they've probably already succeeded. Lastly, make sure your attic is properly ventilated so moisture can't collect and attract dampness-loving insects.

Clothes, especially those stored in closets for long periods, are also very susceptible to pests who prefer munching on fabric away from the harsh glare of the public eye. Here are a few tips for storing bug-friendly items:

1. **Store Garments and Blankets Properly**—Wash or dry-clean items before storage. This will kill any insects in the garments and will make them less appealing for further infestation. If articles are not laundered before storage, at least brush them free of lint in the seams and hang them in the sun for several hours. Store out-of-season garments in tight containers with moth control products to help prevent re-infestation.

2. **Use Moth-proofing Insecticides**—To further protect valuable garments before you store them, use moth-proofing sprays. Make sure to follow all label instructions, so that you don't ruin your clothes. The best way to help prevent damage is to dry-clean clothes before you put them away for the season.

   Note: If you have a heavy infestation of a fabric destroying pest, you should consider making spot applications to areas of carpeting that are under heavy furniture, next to walls, or to areas that receive little foot traffic (you can tell which areas these are because the color of the carpet is the same as it was when you originally picked it out 10 years ago!). Again, follow all label instructions and only use approved products.

3. **Housekeeping**—Frequent cleaning will prevent a buildup of lint and other fibers that attract insects. In fact, vacuuming rugs will not only suck up pests, but whisk away their eggs as well. Be careful, though. Many bugs could put Houdini to shame, and will have no trouble escaping from vacuum bags. Make sure you seal them tightly, and throw them out immediately. Also be sure to thoroughly vacuum heat registers, carpets under heavy furniture, along walls, and areas that do not get much foot traffic.

It's Not the Heat, It's the Humidity

Remember those hair gel ads that used to promote the "wet look?" Well, it may work for hair, but wetness is lousy for your house. The moisture from air conditioning condenses in wall voids, creating fungi that will attract mold-eating insects. From there, insects will make their way into the home, entering through electrical outlets, wall switches, and vents.

Controlling humidity is extremely important and relatively easy to accomplish. Make sure your kitchen, bathroom, utility room, basement, and attic are properly ventilated, and that each vent to the outdoors is not damaged. You should also insulate cold-water pipes and all cold-air ducts of the air conditioning system.

Unfortunately, many of today's homes feature several small rooms as opposed to a few larger rooms. If they're also airtight, that means there's less air around to absorb and disperse the moisture that collects from normal home use. The damper the room and the house, the more you risk infestation by cockroaches, flies, silverfish and/or spiders.

When you've tried everything short of swabbing the walls and floors with a cotton ball to eliminate dampness, you might want to give a dehumidifier a shot. These devices are pretty good at drying up a room and taking away the moisture that attracts insects.

Traps

Another relatively benign way of eliminating pest problems is through the use of traps. Whether you're protecting a tree, or luring a bug into a sticky grave, traps can be a viable alternative to pesticides.

We'll deal with rodents first. While they aren't really a long-term solution for your infestation problems, traps do offer some means of protection from mice and rats. There are three major types of rodent traps: live, snap and glue.

Live traps, as the name implies, capture rodents without killing them. You can buy these products commercially from most major pest control stores or home-supply centers. Simply set them parallel—but an inch away from—the wall and bait them with cheese or some other goody, like pecans. Once you've caught the rodent, set it free far, far away from your home. Never keep these critters as pets and always wear gloves because they may be carrying more diseases than a messenger for Petri Dish, Inc.

The main drawback for the second type of trap—snap traps—is that they have the potential of injuring your pets or children. However, if you can set them in a place where the mammals you love can't reach them, snap traps do a pretty good job of whacking the life out of mice and rats.

Not ones to wait, a female mouse gives birth to six young ones just three weeks after mating. Then she's ready to mate again in two days. She can produce between six to ten litters a year. As if that's not enough, the offspring are ready to mate in two months. One female's children, grandchildren, great-grandchildren, and great, great grandchildren can produce offspring in the same year. Talk about a family reunion! Two mice that began to breed on New Year's Day could theoretically produce over thirty thousand descendants by the end of the year.

If disposing of a potentially messy little carcass disturbs you, you may want to consider glue traps. These traps, which often come pre-baited, snare the rodent in a sticky glue after they go after the lure. You can set these traps in pairs, or under some physical cover so tunnel-loving rats will be more likely to find them. The most common size of glue boards is 5 inches by 7 inches. They can be found at most grocery or hardware stores. For bait, I recommend either cheese, dog food, peanut butter or certain fruits and veggies. Basically, it's a trial-and-error type of thing;

if you have upper-class pests, they may not go for the less expensive lures.

Now, if you were to ask a New Yorker to discuss their favorite roach trap, they might reminisce fondly about a third-floor walk-up on the Lower East Side. However, roaches—along with other indoor pests, such as spiders and flies—can also be captured on glue boards. Make sure to place them in areas where you won't catch your kids. If someone should happen to get stuck, just pour some cooking oil on the glue and it will dissolve.

It is cheaper to buy pre-made glue boards than to try making them yourself. The most famous of these manufactured glue boards is the "roach motel," where the roaches check in, but don't check out. The best way to see which product works best is to simply try out a few different types. If you set a trap in front of a roach and he just laughs and flips you off with all six legs, it's probably time to shop for something else.

In order to control flying insects, you might try flypaper. The most effective products on the market look like a long toilet paper tube that is brightly colored and covered with sticky glue. These tubes are then hung in areas of high fly activity.

Outdoor Treatments

Landscaping in an area known to be "bug-friendly" can be a problem. Sure, you want the outside of your house to look nice, but are you willing to risk your pest-free home to get it? Guests attracted by the pretty exterior of your home will run screaming when they get inside and are attacked by a swarm of blood-thirsty skeeters.

The shrubs and flowers circling your house are pleasing to the eye, but also to the thousands of bug eyes scouting for a good meal or breeding ground. Mites, spiders, ants and cockroaches will show their gratitude for such a fine staging area by barging into your home and making your life hell.

If possible, install a band of pea gravel or sand at least 12 inches wide along the edge or your foundation to act as a barricade against insect entry. Also, try to avoid planting broad-leaved ivies around the perimeter of your home. Their wide, shade-giving leaves provide a fine honeymoon suite for amorous black widow spiders, rats, mice, roaches and carpenter ants.

Preventative maintenance also needs to be done in the yard and garden to hold the pest population to a reasonable level. The lawn should be regularly mowed. Weeds should be pulled and fallen fruits and vegetables removed from the garden. Keep your soil healthy by cultivating gardens during the growing season, and removing plant debris when Old Man Winter shows up.

During the warm, muggy summer nights, flying insects— beetles, mosquitoes, and moths especially—can literally be a pain in the neck. To minimize the problem, you should cut away high weeds and plant debris and regularly clean areas where pests can hide, like under wood decks and on top of storage sheds.

Some metallic wood-boring beetles have a very long larval life, coming out of timber after 40 years.

To ensure that bugs are driven away from your house before they can buzz inside, you might want to consider smoke coils or citronella candles. These products repel insects either through the use of an unpleasant smell or blinding smoke. Both are fairly effective, but only on low-to-moderate infestations. These products are for outside use only. As usual, follow all label instructions carefully.

For bigger invaders such as gophers, rabbits, feral cats and birds, a well-placed stretch of wire mesh, netting or chain-link fence will usually force the critter to raid someone else's garden or else seek intensive animal therapy.

While insects are generally a bigger problem during the summer than the winter, they keep busy during the cold months plotting their revenge for your Insecticide Hoe Down the summer before. Lots of species lay dormant until the temperature rises and you expose your skin for biting again. So don't think that just because you froze your behind off over the winter, the pests did too. Many insects have liquids similar to anti-freeze in their bodies to keep them from freezing.

Where you live can make your pest problem even worse. Mosquitoes, for instance, are more difficult to control in the more heavily wooded suburbs than in the city. And anyone who's vacationed in the South knows that every flying insect in the world has headed that way long before your retired Uncle Stan and Aunt Irene.

As the saying goes, "If you can't stand the heat, get out of the kitchen." Likewise, if you can't stand the skeeters, get out of the swamp.

 In the Garden

Remember those food-chain charts you had to study as a kid in school? The ones which showed how a critter could be a predator one day and somebody's dinner the next? Well, a number of garden pests can be safely eliminated simply by introducing one of their natural enemies into the garden. This is, of course, with the knowledge that the predator insect won't be doing more harm than good to your property.

Aside from the birds, insects, toads and lizards already present in your yard, there are other species you can import to gobble down your pests. Among the most useful insect predators are lacewings, ground beetles, lady beetles, dragonflies, hover flies, miniwasps and centipedes.

Another worthwhile option is a beneficial species of tiny, soil-dwelling roundworms called nematodes. When introduced to your yard, these hungry wrigglers attack white grubs, grasshoppers, Japanese beetles, termites and other pests that reside in the soil.

However, I should tell you, some of these biological controls will take more time, effort, and money to really work. Gardeners have had great success in Great Britain, and some American farmers have been able to control pest populations by introducing predators bought from huge commercial insectaries, but for the layman it's trickier. In some cases, the introduced species doesn't take to its new environment, and just sits around all day taking up space, sort of like your eldest son. Alternatively, they may just fly over to your neighbor's yard.

For the home gardener, I'd probably recommend some lower-tech solutions to your pest problems. For example, sometimes a blast of water or soap-water from a spray can is enough to disable a rampaging bug, or clean off an infested leaf. This method works fairly well for low-grade whitefly infestations. Just spritz those little suckers off your plants! Mites, psyllids, thrips and aphids are also susceptible to simple sprays.

Many times, controlling a garden pest can be as simple as interplanting your trees, shrubs, flowers and other plants in random arrangements, as opposed to straight, even rows or tight clusters. I know that in China, farmers use this method so insects that feed on a particular plant or crop are confined to smaller areas and can't move from plant to plant so easily. It's also easier shooting fish in a barrel than in an ocean, if you get my drift.

You also may want to consider crop rotation to deal with your outdoor pests. If a tomato-loving bug swoops into your garden hoping to grab a table at the same buffet he had last year, imagine his surprise when he's met by yucky squash or strawberries instead.

Also, try to avoid planting heavy concentrations of pest-prone plants like radishes, broccoli, cucumbers and most types of melons. Instead, try such "garden Rambos" as beans, peas and spinach. They can take care of themselves, thank you very much.

Or, you could experiment with something called "trap cropping." Here, we take ultimate advantage of the fact that bugs just ain't too smart. The potato beetle, for instance, happens to like eggplant a heap more than it likes potatoes. So, if you want to protect your potato plants, stick some eggplants across the garden and the potato beetles will do a rhumba right on over there and park it for good.

Need hard workers? Hire some garden fungus termites. They build enormous, rock-hard mounds with sand, clay, and saliva. One such mound contained nearly twelve thousand tons of sand—piled grain by grain.

Another useful strategy for eliminating garden pests is soil solarization. This is basically the braniac way of saying "microwave the suckers." All you have to do is turn over about four inches of topsoil and soak it in water overnight. The next morning, drape a clear, thin plastic tarp over the wet soil and seal the edges tightly, either by staking or burying them in soil. The tarp acts as a greenhouse, trapping heat and destroying harmful bacteria, fungi, insect larvae and weed seeds. Of course, this technique works best in the hottest months of summer. Try this in winter and you'll be putting a cozy electric blanket over your bug bed.

If you're more comfortable in the kitchen than the garden, never fear. A lot of herbs and foods we eat are plum nasty to insects. Remember how your momma told you to ward off vampires with a string of garlic? Well, I'll bet she forgot to mention that it also works on mosquitoes. Come to think of it, they both suck your blood....Anyway, researchers have found that the active ingredient in garlic and onions—allicin—is a pretty darn effective mosquito repellent.

Likewise, planting strong-smelling herbs in your garden like peppermint, wormwood, lavender, rosemary, pennyroyal and sage also keeps bad bugs at bay. The encyclopedia section contains many other herbal strategies.

Humane Live Traps

Various types and brands of traps are available to snare such larger mammals as moles, gophers, raccoons, coyotes, skunks and other more hefty critters. A number of these traps will be detailed later in this book as we discuss control measures on a pest-by-pest basis. Suffice to say, it's a good idea to go to a home-and-garden store, a pest control supply store, or other similarly stocked outlet and examine their choice of traps. Ask the store clerk for more information if you're confused or have any reservations about their use.

CHEMICAL TREATMENTS

IPM strategy doesn't exclude the use of chemicals or pesticides, it simply reserves chemical treatments as a last resort attack against insect infestations. (For the purposes of this book, the terms "chemicals" and "pesticides" will be used interchangeably.) This new approach was developed primarily to combat consumers' increasingly itchy pesticide trigger fingers. Rather than "shoot first, ask questions later," hopefully bug-brained people will now consider 1) Is the pest is a friend or enemy?, 2) If it's an enemy, are there enough of them to warrant preventative measures?, and 3) What are the best, and safest, short- and long-term solutions to the problem? Many times, chemicals or pesticides simply fit the bill as the most prudent choice for pest control.

I think it would be wise to start this chapter by explaining a little bit about what constitutes a chemical or pesticide treatment. A pesticide is a substance, or any mixture of substances, intended for preventing, destroying, or repelling any pest. Pests include insects, animals such as mice, or unwanted plants. Despite the popular belief that all pesticides are insecticides, the term actually refers to herbicides, fungicides and all other substances used to control pests.

Bats may be hated by most people, but they are considered to be the controllers of the insect kingdom. A single bat can eat six hundred mosquito-size insects an hour. In one evening, the average bat colony can consume a half-million insects.

Many household products are pesticides. You may be surprised to learn that all of these items are considered pesticides: cockroach sprays and baits; insect repellents for personal use; rat and other rodent poisons; flea and tick sprays, powders, and pet collars; and certain lawn and garden products, including weed killers.

Because they are designed to kill or in some way adversely effect living organisms, most pesticides do pose some risk of harm to humans, animals, or the environment if not used properly. At the same time, however, we shouldn't overlook their ability to control insects, weeds, and other pests—which actually improves our quality of life in many ways.

The key is determining when to utilize chemicals, in what concentration, and how much to use. An estimated one-third of pesticides used by consumers are wasted, simply because the situation didn't call for it. Not only is this a waste of money, but more importantly, it can be damaging to the environment.

Pesticide residue can linger in soil for a long time. In addition, prolonged or inappropriate use of pesticides can kill beneficial insects and micro-organisms that keep soil rich. A build-up of chemicals in your yard can help to create thatch—bunches of dead grass that result in the smothering of your lawn. This happens after the microbes that decompose grass clippings are destroyed by the excessive use of chemicals on the lawn.

Another major concern is rainwater, which can wash pesticide residue to other areas of your lawn and garden, and into lakes and rivers that supply drinking water. Engineers call this "non-point source" pollution, which is basically contamination from sources such as lawn runoff or dumping—accidental or intentional—of waste into storm sewers.

One area where you should always exercise caution, prudence and self-control is in the home. The rooms where your family eats, sleeps, relaxes and plays are no place to be spraying chemicals haphazardly or without full knowledge of how to use the product. Make sure the product you plan to use is safe to set down or disperse in a sensitive area of your home, before you go ahead and utilize it. Be sure to carefully check all label instructions for proper use and to determine if the product is safe to apply indoors and/or outdoors. Don't be afraid to consult a pest control professional if you have any questions, or if you feel your problem is too large or difficult for you to tackle.

All right. So we know pesticides, if used improperly, aren't good for ourselves or our environment. But, if we use chemicals smart-

Hooray for pest control! Without it, food production would drop by one-third. In developing countries, 50 percent of crops are destroyed by pests when proper control is not practiced. In the United States, the loss is nine percent. When food production drops, prices rise. A 10 percent drop in production can cause retail prices to increase by up to 15 percent. Control measures protect people from many major diseases—including food poisoning, staph infections, rabies, and bubonic plague.

ly—in controlled amounts and in specific situations—and combine this with an ongoing strategy of non-toxic controls, we can solve our pest problems without causing other kinds of damage.

When we use chemicals it is very important to read the *entire* label before you start to apply the product. Unfortunately, most people never do this. However, label warnings are the best way to determine the toxicity of the product you're using. Look for the following designations: "Caution," "Warning," or "Danger." Most products that are ready to use will have the "Caution" label. Concentrates will either have the "Caution" or "Warning" label, depending on their level of toxicity. In either case, make sure you have read all directions thoroughly and have taken the proper precautions before using these products. I would recommend that homeowners not use those chemicals that contain the "Danger" label. Such chemicals should only be handled by a professional exterminator.

Insecticide Formulations

The term "formulation" refers to the form in which a pesticide is packaged and sold. Most products will either be "ready-to-use" or sold as concentrates that you will have to mix with water before using.

The term "concentration"—often seen on the label—refers to the amount of active ingredient that is contained in that particular product. It is calculated by using the percent-by-weight of the active ingredient in comparison to the total formulation of the product itself.

The following are some of the most common liquid and dry pesticide formulations on the market:

Baits—For consumer use, baits usually come in the form of gels, granules, or pastes that are enclosed in covered bait-tray containers. Baits typically use food grade material mixed with a poison. You should be aware that insects are not necessarily bound by law to enter a bait station. It's still a hit-or-miss proposition. Likewise, each kind of bait is designed for a specific type of pest, so don't expect your roaches to realize in psychotherapy that they've always wanted to be slugs, and as a result eat slug bait. They won't. Also, it goes without saying that baits should always be placed out of the reach of children and pets (in the trade we call this "inaccessible").

Botanicals — These are products that are made from plants. The most common one used is pyrethrum, which is derived from a species of Chrysanthemum plant found in Africa.

Dusts — These finely ground, dry formulations come in ready-to-use concentrations when purchased. Dusts are applied to surfaces or in cracks where insects run or hide, and are most effective when used in areas frequented by pests and nothing else. Moisture tends to make dusts less effective. After insects crawl over a dusted area, they inhale the poison or absorb it through their skin. Dusts are, in many cases, more effective than sprays. They are also not flammable and will usually not stain carpet and floors.

Emulsifiable Concentrates — A petroleum-based chemical is mixed with emulsifiers, thus enabling it to be mixed with water. When sprayed on a surface, a chemical residue is laid down that can't normally be seen.

Fumigants — These gaseous pesticides give off vapors that enter the pest's body through inhalation. Active ingredients are sometimes gasses that become liquids when packaged under pressure, and then become gasses again when released during application.

Granules — Larger than dusts, granular particles contain active ingredients that are carried by corncob or clay. The chemical is either coated on the outside of the granules or is absorbed into them. They come ready-to-use and have a low potential for drifting. The granules become active when they get wet. When water makes contact with the granules, the chemical is released in that area and the bugs are killed when they make contact with the treated surface.

Inorganic Insecticides—These are products that are normally mined from mineral deposits. Examples include boric acid, silica aerogel, and diatomaceous earth. They contain no carbon molecule.

Insect Growth Regulators—These chemicals mimic an insect's own juvenile hormone and disrupt normal growth and development. Many products on the market stop the molting process and prevent the stages of metamorphosis. They are usually most successful when used against species with complete metamorphoses like fleas, roaches, mosquitoes and stored-product pests. Variations include methoprene, and hydroprene.

Organophosphates—These chemicals effect the neuromuscular systems of insects and are one of the more common products used in insect control. The primary toxic action of this class of insecticide involves inhibition of cholinesterase, an important enzyme in the nervous system. Disruption of these enzymes eventually causes muscle and organ failure, leading to the death of the insect. Most of these products have a strong odor to them.

Repellents—These are products that repel target pests by emitting a displeasing smell, unpleasant taste or predator odor.

Ready-to-Use Sprays—These can be push-button aerosol cans or non-pressurized products that have a water base and are applied with a hand sprayer. The sprays are formed from a mixture of chemicals, stabilizers and water. Once sprayed on a surface, they will control bugs for 30 to 45 days in most cases.

Spray Solutions—A mixture of water or oil and one or more chemical substances. All of the ingredients dissolve to form a solution.

Wettable Powders—These dry formulations are almost as fine-grained as dusts, however, they contain a higher degree of active ingredients. They must be mixed with water in order to be used. Care must be taken not to breathe the dust while mixing.

Indoor Chemical Treatments

When using chemicals inside the house, you should always first read the entire label to see if the product can be used inside your home, and that it will work effectively on the particular pest you are seeking to eradicate. Most ready-to-use sprays belong to that chemical formulation group that will leave a residual (long-lasting control) for a period of time, usually a little over a month.

If you want to use an organic-type product, look for the active ingredient called "pyrethrum." This product is strictly a contact kill—it does not leave a residual. Many people are having good luck with products that are called "pyrethroids." These products mimic the natural pyrtheum, however they leave a long residual in order to more effectively control bugs.

Probably everyone who's tried to combat home pests has either used—or heard of—two other chemical treatments: foggers and bait stations. The latter are essentially lures enclosed in some sort of trap or housing to attract the pest and then either capture it, or kill it chemically. These stations, if situated in areas where pests can get to them, have a lower impact for home use because they don't disperse chemical powders, dusts or sprays into the air where your family or pets can breathe them. Most bait stations that are on the market are child resistant. However, they still should be placed where children and pets cannot reach them.

Foggers, on the other hand, are a dicier issue. You can kick everyone out of the house, cover all the plants and furniture and hope you don't ruin anything, but a lot of items around the house will still get unnecessarily treated with chemicals. Normally, I don't recommend foggers for inside the house. Yes! Yes! I know they're easy to use, but the only place I like to use foggers is in the attic, at the beginning of spring and fall. Just make sure to turn off any pilot lights.

There are also a wide variety of rodenticides—chemicals used to kill mice and rats—that are available commercially. Read labels carefully, or consult a pest control specialist, to determine if and when to use these products. Be sure to choose the chemical formulation that will not only be most effective on your rodent problem, but more importantly, safest for home use.

In addition to pyrethrin insecticides, boric acid, DE, hydramethylnon, and Fipronil are commonly acknowledged as good low-impact chemical controls against such pests as cockroaches, ants, and silverfish.

Under ideal conditions one female cockroach can give birth to two million babies in a year. The average breeding season produces thirty five thousand little ones.

Boric acid seems to work in two ways: one, by penetrating the insect's outer covering; and, two, by collecting on the insect's feet, then getting swallowed when the insect preens itself. Sold commercially under various brand names like Roach Prufe, boric acid has been around for a long time and, when used properly,

The taste receptors of some insects are on their feet. How appetizing!

generates good results. In fact, many insects have developed immunities to many other controls, but not boric acid.

To apply boric acid, sprinkle a small film of the chemical in out-of-the-way places where insects come and go, but your family doesn't. The use of a bulb duster will make your application of the product an easier task. Then be prepared to wait the insects out. Boric acid takes longer to work than some other chemicals, but that doesn't mean it's lying down on the job. It should take anywhere from two days to two weeks before you notice the insect population has thinned considerably.

Because the chemical is toxic, you should never disperse it in food-storage areas. Likewise, never sprinkle it where people walk. The acid is extremely slippery and may put more of your friends and family out of commission than the insects. Also, when using the product, make sure to wear gloves and a surgical-type mask to avoid any contact with, or inhalation of, the chemical. This is a good habit to get into when using all dust formulations.

Hydramethylnon, sold in stores as Combat, is much newer to the pest control scene than boric acid. While the latter was in use even at the turn of the century, the former has been around for about 12 years. Because hydramethylnon is effective in much smaller quantities than boric acid, some professionals feel Combat is a better product choice when going after ants or roaches.

Also, because the chemical in its containerized form doesn't blow around or scatter like boric acid, it can be used in food shelves, kitchen drawers and other places where you should never apply boric acid. If used properly and in regularly cleaned areas free from loose food products, Combat should start decreasing your roach or ant population in about a week.

Outdoor Chemical Treatments

A wide spectrum of chemicals are available for use on outdoor pests. However, don't go on the assumption that just because you're using them outside, it's okay to dump whatever chemicals you want into the soil, or spray nine cans of flying insect killer into the air or foliage of a tree. Common sense should tell you that many of the same risks to humans are present out of doors as they are indoors.

Adding to the threat to our respiratory systems and skin surfaces from garden pesticides, there's also the environmental issues. As I mentioned earlier in this chapter, soil contamination from yard chemical use can linger longer than you want. Also, rainwater runoff will often transport pesticide residue into lakes, rivers and drinking water supplies. I'm repeating these warnings only to emphasize the real need for caution when using chemicals—indoor or out.

One relatively low impact garden product is the soil bacterium *bacillus thuringiensis*, also called "BT." It is primarily used to control moth larvae. The bacteria works by producing a number of biological poisons called "endotoxins," which are released from a protein housing by the acids in a caterpillar's gut. Because few other insects have such acidic insides, BT can be sprayed on caterpillar-infested plants with little danger that other bugs will be affected. Despite being caterpillar Kryptonite, BT is almost non-toxic to mammals. At worst, the bacterium is a minor eye and skin irritant.

Two other fairly benign garden chemicals are horticultural oils and insecticidal soap. These products are applied directly to infested plants and act as a layer of protection for susceptible leaves, stems and branches. However, you need to be careful as these sprays can sometimes cause sensitive foliage to turn yellow or die. Read product labels closely, and experiment on one or two leaves first before applying to the whole plant, bush or tree.

Basically, horticultural oil works by covering the stems of deciduous woody plants and suffocating pests like aphids, thrips, spider mites, scale, and mealybugs. It also smothers most over-wintering eggs or larvae.

Movie Review

Slugs (1987)—Here's a premise I can almost believe. The government is using slugs to clean up—surprise again!!—toxic waste, when to the horror of the Department of the Interior, the slugs mutate into bloodthirsty man-eaters. Has anyone in Hollywood ever seen a slug make its way across a garden? These suckers move about a mile a month, and here in this flick we've got people running like the dickens to escape them to no avail. Excuse me, but let's have just a little realism here, huh?

(All reviews are on a scale of 1 to 5 roaches, with 5 being best.)

When insecticidal soaps are used, they kill the insect by penetrating the exoskeleton, causing the pest to die from dehydration. A product such as "Safer Insecticidal Soap," when used properly, kills soft-bodied insects—for instance, aphids—more quickly than such hard-shelled pests as beetles.

Insecticidal soap works essentially the same way, but contains insecticidal chemical formulations as opposed to horticultural varieties. When using either of these products, apply only to the infested parts of the plants, and always use a dust mask, or other safety equipment, when spraying.

Molluscicide is the term used to describe chemicals that specifically kill snails and slugs. Currently, there are basically two chemicals used as molluscicides: methiocarb and metaldehyde. They work by acting on both brain and neural systems to inhibit the urge to feed. The creatures literally starve to death. While the debate rages on about which of the two chemicals is the better slimer killer, both have been proven to be equally effective baits.

Methiocarb and Metaldehyde are toxic to mammals if swallowed, and a skin and eye irritant if contacted to these surfaces. It also appears to be highly toxic to many fish and birds. Needless to say, extreme caution should be taken when using these chemicals. Always read and follow label instructions carefully.

CHAPTER 6

SAFETY

Tips On Using Pesticides Safely and Effectively

1. **Minimize your exposure to the product.** When you use a chemical to control your pest problem, make spot applications and limit your contact with the chemical as much as possible. Stay away from treated surfaces until dry.

2. **Store products safely and in their original containers.** Regardless of a chemical's toxicity, it should be stored in a locked cabinet, high shelf or a place impossible for children or pets to reach. Never leave toxic materials under a kitchen or bathroom sink, even if securely latched or bolted.

3. **Wear protective clothing.** Whether it's a face shield, safety goggles, rubber gloves, respirator, safety helmet, rubber apron, or even something as simple as a wide-brimmed hat, make sure you're wearing the right gear for the products you're handling. Remember, it's always best to be over-prepared when dealing with chemicals.

4. **Avoid overkill.** Sometimes, a less toxic product is all you need to combat your pest problems.

5. **Follow guidelines for areas of use.** Never apply an outdoor product on indoor pests. The label says "for outdoor use only" for a reason. For example, some outdoor products, if used indoors, could discolor your carpet.

6. **Take precautions before spraying.** Work in an area with plenty of ventilation, and cover all food products and pet dishes. Never spray on food preparation areas, and if "fogging" an attic, make sure to turn off all pilot lights in the attic.

7. **Keep children and pets out of the house.** Most children and pets are persistent in their curiosity. If possible, keep them out of the house until treated areas are dry. Remember: it always pays to be overly cautious when dealing with pesticides.

8. **Use caution when opening a product.** Never use your hands to tear open a chemical housed in a paper sack; always use a knife, or other sharp-edged cutting tool. When opening a can or container of liquid, hold it as far below your eyes as possible and turn your face away until the cap or lid is safely off.

9. **Take note of wind conditions.** Never spray an outdoor chemical when a hard wind is blowing. Not only will your infested areas not receive enough product, but the spray will drift into your neighbor's yard.

10. **Never smoke when using a pesticide.** This is a given, but I thought I'd mention it anyway in case the Marlboro Man finds a few cheese skippers in his pantry.

Child Safety

Nearly half of all households with children under the age of five have at least one pesticide in an unlocked storage area less than four feet off the ground. Even if you don't have children, you should still store your pest control products safely. Almost 75 percent of households without small children keep pesticides in an unlocked storage area less than four feet off the ground. This is significant because 13 percent of all children poisoned by pesticides occur in homes other than where the child lives.

Kitchens and bathrooms are the most likely rooms to find improperly stored chemicals such as insect and wasp sprays, roach sprays, rat poisons, and flea and tick shampoos and dips for pets. If possible, store your pesticides in a locked cabinet, where children cannot reach them.

If your use of a pesticide is interrupted—such as by the telephone ringing or a knock on the door—properly close the package and put it out of the reach of children while you are gone.

Never place pesticides in containers that children associate with food or drink. Teach your children that pesticides are poisons and should never be tampered with, even in fun. Inform others about the potential hazard of pesticides, particularly caregivers and grandparents, and keep the telephone number of your area poison control center close to the phone in case of emergency.

Emergency First Aid Guidelines

If someone is improperly exposed to a harmful pesticide, try to determine which part or parts of the body are affected and by which chemical. Should the person be unconscious, experience difficulty breathing, or have convulsions, call 911 or your local emergency service immediately.

If the person does not have clearly identifiable symptoms, contact your local poison control center, doctor, 911, or local emergency service and follow their instructions. Try to have the product container with you when you call.

Here are some guidelines for more specific exposures:

Swallowed Poison—Induce vomiting only if emergency personnel on the phone instruct you to do so. Usually, it depends on what the person has swallowed. Vomiting actually makes the problem worse if certain petroleum products or caustic poisons have been ingested. If instructed to do so, induce vomiting with Syrup of Ipecac. Always store Syrup of Ipecac out of the reach of children, and make sure the product hasn't passed its use-by date.

Poison in the Eye—Eye damage can occur in a few minutes after exposure to some types of pesticides, faster than any other external part of the body. If poison should splash into an eye, hold the eyelid open and wash quickly and gently with clean, running tap water or a gentle stream from a hose for at least 15 minutes. If possible, have someone else contact the poison control center or emergency personnel while the victim is being treated.

Poison on Skin—Should pesticides splash on the skin, drench the exposed area with water and immediately remove contaminated clothing. If stinging persists or a rash develops, contact your doctor or poison control center immediately.

Inhaled Poison—Remove the victim to an area with fresh air at once. Should you feel you're at risk entering the contaminated area, call 911 or the local fire department first before proceeding. Once it is safe to approach the scene, loosen the victim's clothing, and determine if the victim's skin is blue or if breathing has stopped. If so, give artificial respiration if you've been accredited to do so, or call 911 or your local emergency service for help. Be sure to immediately ventilate the area so no one else will be poisoned by the fumes.

 # When To Call a Professional

Even though I'm a pest control operator (PCO) myself, I can remain objective when it comes to the right and wrong times to call a professional out to your house for a bug problem. After all, anyone can lay down a few roach stations, if that's the solution to your insect troubles.

But I hope you also realize that it's one thing to crawl under your sink and work on a drain instead of calling a plumber, and another to handle chemicals yourself instead of hiring an expert. This is no time to be brave, macho or cheap. If you don't feel confident treating your pest problem on your own, it's worth the extra few dollars to bring in a PCO rather than bungling the job yourself.

More than anything, it's a question of common sense. Do you have the time and patience to do the job right? Have you handled pesticides before? Is this a small insect problem, or a full-scale infestation? Do you even recognize the species of insect you're trying to control? Do you have to treat attics, behind walls or in other hard-to-reach places?

All these questions are important to answer before you decide to do the job yourself. That being said, I think that most pest control jobs are, in theory, manageable by a non-professional. National statistics show that over 75% of the population practices some sort of pest control eradication on their own. If you're adamant about reading as much as you can about the insect you're hunting and the type of methods necessary to control it; if you are not above calling and asking a professional for advice; if you make sure to read and follow all the instructions and warnings on the products you use; and, if you are able to successfully utilize non-toxic control methods as well, then I applaud your efforts and wish you well.

There's only one type of infestation that I absolutely, positively insist you leave to a PCO. And that's termites in structures that have already been built. PCOs have the knowledge and the equipment to do the job properly.

Here are a few more advantages of PCOs:

- PCOs are licensed, certified, and insured.

- PCOs are trained to follow all local, county, state, and national laws.

- PCOs can identify the invaders that are attacking your home, and can also recommend the best way to get rid of them.

- PCOs can advise you on how to make your home and yard less attractive to future pest invaders.

- PCOs have access to a wider selection of effective pesticides than consumers.

- PCOs will work in difficult climatic conditions.

- PCOs provide valuable advice and information on pesticides.

- PCOs follow strict environmental guidelines.

- PCOs have the equipment—accurate sprayers, granule spreaders, and precision injection tools—needed to effectively deal with perimeter invaders.

But, if you take the necessary precautions to ensure your home is not attractive to bugs, you may never need to call us out in the first place. So, if you hit upon an effective way to control your pest problem naturally, safely and efficiently, we'll happily stay home and watch football.

CHAPTER 7

ENCYCLOPEDIA OF HOME AND GARDEN PESTS

At this point in the book, we're going to go species by species, variety by variety, and talk about the best and safest ways to eliminate each pest. I hope you've been paying attention, class. And remember your IPM strategy:

1. Identify your pest problem.

2. Know the pest's biology.

3. Determine the parameters of your action threshold.

4. Use the most effective and safest pest-management plan.

If one thing sticks in your mind from this book, I hope it's that we're trying to do everything in our power to safely eradicate our home and garden pests. If you must handle a pest problem chemically, make sure you take every possible precaution to ensure you're using the products safely, or call a professional.

Now that I've got my preachin' out of the way, let's get rid of "What's Buggin' You!"

❊ How to Use the Size Range Scale ❊

Before you can control the pest that's buggin' you, you have to be able to figure out exactly what it is. To that end, I've provided you with an illustration of the pest, general information to help you identify it, and a nifty little scale. All you have to do is hold up your critter to the bar to see if its size falls within the range shown. In the example given, a mud dauber wasp can be anywhere from 1 to 1½ inches long, so the black bar goes up to 1 inch, and then the striped area, indicating the range, goes up to 1½ inches. Clear enough? Good! Oh, and one other note: In the case of pests who are too big to fit onto the page—or so small that you'd need a microscope to see them—I've simply listed the size without the aid of a scale. After all, do you really want to try holding an armadillo against the pages of this book?

Mud Dauber Wasp

Size Range:

| 0 | | 1 | 1½ | 2 |

Size to scale in inches

ANTS

L iving by the adage "early to bed and early to rise," ants get much of their work done in the morning. But just like people, there are variations. Certain worker ants have a seemingly endless supply of energy, while others are lazy. Climate also plays a role, as ants seem to have a high level of activity in midsummer, and stay dormant in the winter months.

Ants are social insects and live in well-organized colonies, kind of like college fraternities, but without the kegs, hazing and bad '70s rock music. The worker adults—the stage of the ant life cycle on view for humans—hunt for food, and are capable of finding their way through complicated mazes. If you spot a line of workers, it probably means the nest is not far away.

Once a food source is found, the scout ant will leave a clear pheromone trail on his way back to the colony. Other worker ants follow this trail like signposts to the food. That is why many times you will see lines of ants going to the food source and then back to the nest.

Colonies of some species contain upwards of a million ants, with one or sometimes many queens in charge of things. In order to eradicate the entire colony, you must kill all the queens (although you might want to keep a few around if you happen to be playing poker later that evening).

A quick tip: if you've gone through every ant control technique in the book and just can't get rid of the critters, try planting a little peppermint. Ants hate the stuff.

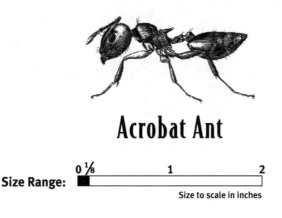

Acrobat Ant

Size Range: 0 ⅛   1   2

Size to scale in inches

IDENTIFICATION & GENERAL INFORMATION

This small ant is two-toned in color, with a light brown front half and dark brown or black rear half. It's easy to identify by its heart-shaped abdomen. With the help of magnification, you can see one pair of spines on its thorax. The acrobat ant is attracted to areas of moisture and likes to crawl on moisture-saturated wood. It likes to nest in the foam insulation in the outside walls of many homes. If you find small piles of insulation on your window sills, the mess was probably caused by acrobat ants.

PREVENTATIVE & LOW-IMPACT TREATMENT

Because this pest is attracted to moisture, take care that your foundation, and especially all exposed wood, is kept dry. Also, dispose of any cluttered piles of wood that may be laying around your property attracting ants. If there are stray logs, boards, beams, or any other wood product strewn about your yard picking up moisture, you're just asking for acrobat ant problems.

CHEMICAL TREATMENT

Since this ant nests many times inside the outer wall voids of homes, this is where you should use an insecticide. Watch where the ants enter your home. Use an aerosol with a narrow crack and crevice applicator similar to what is found on WD-40. I like to use a pyrethrum aerosol and then follow up with a dust-like boric acid or DE. For eradication of exterior populations, treat the foundation with a residual insecticide.

A granular bait called Maxforce works well. You should be able to buy it from a pest control specialty store, listed in the Yellow Pages under "Pest Control Supplies." This is an outdoor bait that the ants take back to their nest. Within a week, the entire colony should be exterminated. When using this bait, do not use any type of spray or dust—it will prevent the ants from carrying the bait back to the nest.

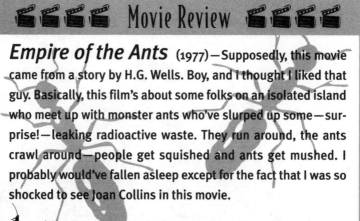

Movie Review

Empire of the Ants (1977)—Supposedly, this movie came from a story by H.G. Wells. Boy, and I thought I liked that guy. Basically, this film's about some folks on an isolated island who meet up with monster ants who've slurped up some—surprise!—leaking radioactive waste. They run around, the ants crawl around—people get squished and ants get mushed. I probably would've fallen asleep except for the fact that I was so shocked to see Joan Collins in this movie.

(All reviews are on a scale of 1 to 5 roaches, with 5 being best.)

Argentine Ant

Size: 1/16 inch long.

IDENTIFICATION & GENERAL INFORMATION

This small, brownish ant spends most of its time outdoors, but can invade homes. The Argentine ant likes to nest in moist, highly organic areas next to building foundations. The species enjoys sweet things, and will go so far as to "farm" aphids on plant leaves in order to milk their "honeydew" for food. Argentine ants like to hide under rocks and wood stacked on the ground next to the house. As a result, large numbers of these ants will enter your home when it is either too dry or too wet outside.

PREVENTATIVE & LOW-IMPACT TREATMENT

Trim your yard and perimeter bushes away from the walls of your house. Pick up any boards or rocks on the ground under which the ants could nest, and fill all foundation and wall cracks with a good silicone caulk.

Because this species is fond of sweets, make sure to remove or secure any outdoor plant that produces a sweet fruit or nectar. Inside, keep candies and sweets properly stored. In other words, don't leave a half-eaten Snickers out for the dog.

CHEMICAL TREATMENT

Use a liquid-residual insecticide, taking care to treat the lower part of your foundation. Pay particular attention to rocks and boards stacked on the ground. If you have weep holes, dust them with an approved residual-type dust. Should the ants try to get inside your home, use bait stations. When using baits, make sure that the label specifically states that it works on Argentine ants or else you're wasting your money.

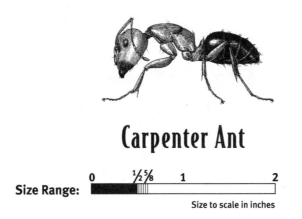

Carpenter Ant

Size Range:

0   ½ ⅝   1   2

Size to scale in inches

IDENTIFICATION & GENERAL INFORMATION

These longish ants have large, shiny heads and, depending on what part of the country you live in, are either solid black in color or half-red, half-black. During spring, the reproductives will develop wings and can be seen at window sills. Carpenter ants are polymorphic, meaning the size of the ants in the colony will vary from small to large.

Carpenter ants do not eat wood like termites, but they will eat almost anything else. However, ironically, they cause the most damage by tunneling in wood—both outdoors and indoors—and making large, "sculptured" nest cavities. It is the smooth, sandpaper-like finish of these galleries that gives these ants their name.

PREVENTATIVE & LOW-IMPACT TREATMENT

Start by eliminating potential nesting spots outdoors. Remove stumps, piles of firewood or buried wood that may contain the moisture these ants need to thrive. Indoors, do everything possible to eliminate moisture buildup in infested areas. Repair leaks in the walls and roof, correct drainage problems and make sure pipe fittings are water-tight.

If you can't locate the outdoor nest, try to close off any potential entry points to your home. Prevent tree branches from touching any walls, and plug any entry points—pipes, electrical lines or loose window frames—with caulk or some other substance.

CHEMICAL TREATMENT

Watch where these ants travel. The key to controlling them is the application of insecticides to the nest area. If you see a compound called "frass" (ant sawdust mixed in with dead ant parts), the nest is close by. The injection of dusts or aerosols into such void areas is needed. To introduce product behind the wall, use small tubes made for this purpose. Also, look for holes on outside walls.

Spraying the foundation where the carpenter ants have concentrated will help prevent future reinfestations.

The dusts of choice would be DE with pyrethrum or boric acid. Using the proper hand duster or aerosol with a tip similar to that found on WD-40 spray will allow you to effectively treat wall voids. Baits such as Maxforce granular also work well. Small amounts of bait should be put in areas of outside ant activity. Do not spray or dust when using this bait.

Once the ants find the bait, they feed it to the entire ant colony. Baiting for two or three days should eradicate the colony. Note: Ant bait stations don't effectively get rid of carpenter ants; they prefer a loose type of bait. I prefer baiting instead of spraying or using aerosols or dusts.

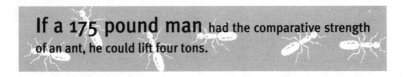

If a 175 pound man had the comparative strength of an ant, he could lift four tons.

Crazy Ant

Size: 1/16 to 1/8 inch long.

IDENTIFICATION & GENERAL INFORMATION

This small brown ant has very long legs compared to the rest of its body. It is called "crazy" because of the haphazard way it walks when searching for food. Rainy weather forces it indoors, where it is usually found on kitchen or bathroom countertops.

PREVENTATIVE & LOW-IMPACT TREATMENT

Because this is primarily an outdoor pest, the key to avoiding indoor infestations is to seal all entry points to your home. Screen all your windows and vents, and seal cracks and crevices in your foundation and around doors. As mentioned earlier, watch out for lines of invading ants when heavy precipitation may disturb the ants' nest and force them to seek shelter in your humble abode.

CHEMICAL TREATMENT

Use a residual liquid chemical, and spray a barrier at the base of the house to prevent reinfestation. Since this ant lives in wall voids, these areas need to be dusted. Make sure to dust the areas under the sink where the plumbing goes into the walls. Note: *Do not* treat food preparation areas.

On countertops, use bait stations that contain the active ingredient Fipronil or hydramethylnon. Using DE or boric acid, dust all weep holes and plumbing voids under sinks. Treating the outside foundation with a residual chemical will prevent reinfestation; micro-encapsulated residuals work the best.

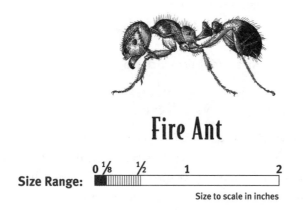

Fire Ant

Size Range: 0 ⅛   ½   1   2

Size to scale in inches

IDENTIFICATION & GENERAL INFORMATION

While some colonies nest under boards, rocks and plants, most form large nest mounds in open ground. This red and black ant becomes very aggressive when its mound is disturbed; it will rush out and repeatedly sting you. The sting burns like fire, hence the name "fire ant." Since the average mound contains more than 5,000 ants, use extreme caution when disturbing the nest. Because they can't survive in extreme cold weather, most fire ant species are found in the warmer climates of the United States.

PREVENTATIVE & LOW-IMPACT TREATMENT

Beneficial nematodes are an option. As I mentioned earlier, they are microscopic, soil-dwelling worms that destroy the fire ants. The brand I have used with good results is Antidote. Nematodes must be refrigerated prior to use.

For a quick short-term control method, simply pour a gallon of boiling water into the middle of the mound. Early-to-mid morning, when the ground is warm but not hot, is the best time for this treatment as most of the colony will be just under the mound surface.

CHEMICAL TREATMENT

Three types of products are available: chemical "drenches," "baits" and "dusts." The drench method works the fastest. Using an approved insecticide, mix the concentrate with water and pour onto the mound. Take care not to step on, or collapse the mound in any way.

Bait formulations like Amdro contain hydramethylnon and are a low-toxicity choice. Treat around mounds in the early morning or late evening hours on dry days. Store bait in a secure, cool part of the house (the garage is too hot in the summer).

The most common dust is Orthene (active ingredient: acephate). It has a strong odor, but is an inexpensive way to control mounds. Follow label instructions closely, applying the dust to the top of the mound, without disturbing the mound itself. Do not treat mounds next to the house with this product, as the strong odor may enter the house.

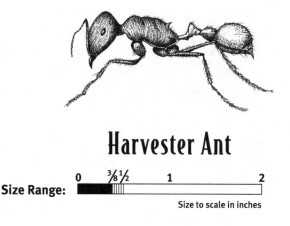

Harvester Ant

Size Range:

0   ⅜½   1   2

Size to scale in inches

IDENTIFICATION & GENERAL INFORMATION

This ant is brown to black in color, and easily identifiable by a "beard" of hair found behind its head and on its underside. These extra tufts of hair help it carry food to the nest. The entrance to the nest is easy to spot because it will be free of any type of vegetation. This outdoor ant, which feeds mainly on grasses, is most likely to be found in rural areas. Be careful: the harvester ant has a stinger and he ain't afraid to use it!

PREVENTATIVE & LOW-IMPACT TREATMENT

As with other outdoor ants, there are a few basic preventative measures you can use to proactively eliminate infestation. First of all, make sure that all outdoor harborages like rotting wood, firewood piles or old play equipment are either discarded or secured in a sealed shed.

Also, create a non-organic barrier between your lawn or garden and the foundation of your home. Use either concrete, pea gravel, or some other material that will provide a "moat" of protection between the infested area and your home. As always, make sure all potential entry points to your home are sealed and impenetrable. Build out these ants.

CHEMICAL TREATMENT

Mound drenching with an approved insecticide will give partial control, but this may not be the most effective treatment considering the extensive nature of their underground galleries.

Also, baits do a very good job of controlling this ant. Don't pile it at the entrance of the nest—spread it out two to four feet from the opening. Follow all instructions carefully.

Little Black Ant

Size: 1/16 inch long.

IDENTIFICATION & GENERAL INFORMATION

This very small ant is jet black in color and very similar to the pharaoh ant in size. Under low magnification, you can see two nodes on its petiole—the stalk-like part between the thorax and abdomen. Obviously, this species doesn't have the cash to get these unsightly blemishes lanced. Like fire ants, little black ants will make a small mound of loose dirt in a yard or garden area. Many times, I have found this ant living in potted plants on the patio. It will feed on almost anything from proteins to carbohydrates.

PREVENTATIVE & LOW-IMPACT TREATMENT

Keep a one-to-two foot area around your home free of debris and trash. Move woodpiles away from the foundation, and apply a good silicone caulk to cracks and crevices on your foundation.

If you must have potted plants on your porch, or close to your house, inspect them regularly for signs of ant infestation, or make sure that the little black ant has no way to scoot from your begonia to your bedroom unimpeded.

Look for the loose-dirt mounds in your yard that may signal an infestation and try to determine why this place is so attractive for the ants. Is there a ready source of foodstuffs close by? Is the ant mound cable-ready? Sometimes, using common sense can eradicate an ant problem before it spills over into your home.

CHEMICAL TREATMENT

To destroy the nest, use a liquid drench. This gets the material quickly into the core of the nest. Make spot treatments to individual nests.

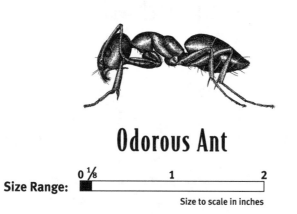

Odorous Ant

Size Range:

0 ⅛   1   2

Size to scale in inches

IDENTIFICATION & GENERAL INFORMATION

This black-colored ant gets its name from the foul smell given off when it is smashed. If you do happen to smash it when company's over, just blame the dog. Most infestations of this species occur in the spring and near kitchen sinks, especially on outside walls and countertops. When disturbed, the ants move in an erratic pattern.

Preventative & Low-Impact Treatment

Trim bushes next to the house, leaving a good air barrier between your yard and foundation. Store all firewood off the ground, and always check the logs for signs of infestation before bringing them into the house.

Take care to remove any and all potential outdoor nesting sites. These include piles of leaves, old 2 x 4s laying around by your foundation, rotting playtoys or athletic equipment, and bags of improperly sealed garbage left out for trash day.

Because most odorous ant activity in the home occurs near kitchen and bathroom sinks, make sure that counters and stove tops are frequently wiped, and kept clean of food products and excessive moisture.

Chemical Treatment

Since this is an outside-invading ant, the best control is to use a micro-encapsulated insecticide at the base of your home. Treat the area from ground level to about a foot up the sides of the house. Make sure to treat all cracks and crevices. If you have a slab-foundation home, dust all weep holes.

Using either boric acid or DE with pyrethrum, take a hand duster and treat all plumbing voids under the sinks, as well as weep holes and any cracks in caulking at the lower parts of window sills. The placement of approved bait stations on the countertops will knock off the rest of the ants. Control is not quick; it may take several weeks.

Remember, if you stomp on these critters, you may have to light a match and explain to everyone how you really didn't have Mexican food for lunch.

Pharaoh Ant

Size: 1/16 inch long.

IDENTIFICATION & GENERAL INFORMATION

A yellowish-brown-colored ant. Most of the time, this species will be found on the kitchen countertop, near the sink or on pantry shelves. These ants are found inside the home when it's very hot outside, or when it's very cold. Pharaoh ants like to travel in a line, accomplished by laying down a pheromone trail for the other ants to follow. This species' nest—usually housing well over 100,000 ants—is found inside a wall or door void. Only five-percent of the colony, however, forages for food. The rest of them have to lift those huge palm fronds and fan the pharaoh. Just kidding.

PREVENTATIVE & LOW-IMPACT TREATMENT

Because pharaohs prefer warm, moist areas, try to keep hot water pipes and other heat sources in tightly secured areas, and check them often for signs of ant activity.

Labeled baits are also available that can be placed on countertops, without fear of contaminating food or other household products. Control usually takes between one and two weeks. I like to attach the bait stations above an electrical plug, which the ants use as a highway. 12 to 16 baits are typically needed. Look for baits that contain hydramethylnon or fipronil.

CHEMICAL TREATMENT

There is none. People who spray to control this ant are making the problem worse. Use of any type of insecticide causes the colony to split and more ants will appear. Do not spray!

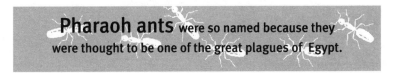

Pharaoh ants were so named because they were thought to be one of the great plagues of Egypt.

APHIDS

A few aphids on your roses shouldn't be enough to send you to a garden psychologist. Most plants can sustain a moderate number of these pear-shaped little pests without harm. However, if they proliferate, aphids can cause leaves to turn yellow or curl, while the plant itself grows weaker and weaker trying to defend itself.

The insects' piercing mouthparts allow them to suck plant juices from not only leaves, but also stems, flowers and fruits. Aphid activity is most prominent in the early spring and fall, and usually is centered on a plant's growing tips.

If you do decide to rid your garden of aphids, you'll have plenty of help. These critters have a busload of natural predators, including lacewings, lady beetles, daddy longlegs spiders and praying mantises. Ants also find aphids quite tasty. Making aphid life even worse are natural controls like temperature extremes, hard rains, fungi and bacterial diseases. Amazingly, over 4,000 species of aphids have been recorded.

Aphid

Size: 1/16 to 1/8 inch long.

IDENTIFICATION & GENERAL INFORMATION

Most aphids are green, but some are pink, brown or black. In addition to long antennae, two little tube-like nodes stick out from the rear of the bug's abdomen. Because of their short life cycle, aphids can multiply rapidly. The first aphid hatchling of the spring—the stem mother—then gives birth to live daughters which in turn have their own daughters. All this reproduction is asexual, so the male aphids will usually be found in a local bar or peep show. At the end of fall, aphids produce winged males and females, which mate, disperse eggs and die. Curiously, this pattern is very similar to the life cycles in the musical group Menudo.

PREVENTATIVE & LOW-IMPACT TREATMENT

To expose aphids to harsh weather and predators, thin out the dense undergrowth of tree material that provides the insects with secure living quarters. This will force the bugs out into the open, where they become some other critter's light snack. To make sure that enough of these natural enemies are around, plant wildflowers and a few weedy species at the garden border to attract aphid-eaters.

If you can't find another insect to do the dirty work, pick up a hose or spray bottle and wash the suckers off leaves and plant growing tips with a concentrated stream of plain or soapy water. Pruning the infested plant parts also helps.

If you prefer a more hands-on approach, you can either rub the affected leaves gently between your thumb and forefinger, or wipe the plant with a damp cloth.

A number of garden herbs are also fairly effective for driving off aphids. These include chives, pennyroyal, coriander, petunia and spearmint.

CHEMICAL TREATMENT

I generally don't recommend using pesticides to control aphids. What usually ends up happening is the chemicals kill the good predators, as well as the aphids

If you insist on using pesticides, follow all instructions carefully. Give the aphids' natural predators some time to do the job for you before you blast 'em with the serious stuff. Then, use only the most benign products like insecticidal soap or a light horticultural oil.

ARMADILLOS

B eing overweight and having short legs has never kept the nine-banded armadillo from its appointed rounds. The armadillo moves quickly and can dig a hole in record time. Technically known as the *Dasypus novemcinctus*, it is the sole variety of this mammal in the United States, and can be found in Arkansas, Mississippi, Georgia, southern Oklahoma, Texas, Louisiana, and parts of Florida.

The three-banded, six-banded, and giant armadillos are found in South America. These varieties range in size from just six inches to nearly a yard long (excluding the tail) when fully grown. All these bands probably explain why armadillos are found out on the road so much.

These squatty animals can be a great help because they feed on pests such as spiders, scorpions, termites, roaches and fire ants. But they can also become pests, damaging lawns and gardens in their quest for food. In addition, they can weaken building foundations, destroy water levees and dig holes in fields that are a danger to animals and farm equipment.

While armadillos are nocturnal, they can occasionally be spotted during the day. Young ones are born in February through April—always four babies at a time, and all the same sex. The babies have a soft coat of armor, which doesn't harden until they are fully grown.

The reason why so many armadillos are killed on the road is that when a car's headlights startle them on the road, they jump up about two feet in the air—about the same height as the front grill of the car. Adios amigo!

Nine-Banded Armadillo

Size: 1 to 2 1/2 feet long; 7 to 15 pounds.

IDENTIFICATION & GENERAL INFORMATION

This animal is easy to identify by its pig-like nose and well protected "horny" outer covering. Wait a sec. I've actually just
described every male fan I've ever seen at a Cowboys game. Suffice it to say, these animals are one-of-a-kind. Most armadillo dens
are six to eight inches wide and may extend more than 20 feet
below the surface of the ground.

PREVENTATIVE & LOW-IMPACT TREATMENT

Trapping is about all you can do, but be prepared: armadillos are
difficult to catch. A typical raccoon trap, measuring 32 x 10 x 12
inches should work, although in some cases you may need to use
a two-door model that is larger and longer. I have had good luck
with the Tomahawk trap model 108.7 (it is 48 x 10 x 12 inches
and is specially reinforced). Since armadillos are creatures of
habit, all you'll need to do is place a trap in their pathway.

With a two-door trap, you won't need bait. To help funnel the
animal inside the trap, use long pieces of scrap wood to form
"wings." When using a single door trap, the best bait is a unique

combination: nightcrawlers hung in a nylon stocking. Be careful, though, because you might snare a few of your neighbors while you're at it. Another option is nearly rotten fruit, such as pears or cantaloupe.

Also, just about any model of American-made sedan is also a proven armadillo squisher if they happen to be scooting across your local roadway.

Chemical Treatment

A new product is now available called Dr. T's Whole. It is a 100% castor oil product that is sprayed on bedding and grass areas to help discourage armadillos from digging for worms and insects.

BATS

B ats have gotten a bad rap. Contrary to popular belief, only a small percentage of them have rabies. Furthermore, bats are not blind; they can see perfectly well in bright light. They're also the only mammals that truly fly (if you don't count the late Jerry Garcia).

Experts recognize that bats are very beneficial to society. Bat dung, often called "guano," is used as fertilizer. Bats also pollinate plants and feed on insects. A single brown bat can digest 1,000 insects a night.

There are about 800 known species of bats, with 40 of them found in the United States. Thirty-two species have been recorded in Texas alone, with the cave bat and Mexican free-tail bat being the most common. The largest bat species is the flying fox, which has a wing span measuring up to five feet.

There are two suborders of bats, *Megachiroptera* (greater bats) and *Microchiroptera* (lesser bats). Some people also include Louisville Sluggers.

Bats can be found everywhere except an area north of the Arctic Circle in Asia, the treeless regions of Greenland and northern Canada, and Antarctica. These high-flying mammals make their homes in dark, secluded places such as caves, attics and church steeples. Most bats sleep during the day, suspended upside down, clinging to a roost with their feet.

Ever wonder why bats insist on hanging upside down? Because it's convenient! By hanging down, they can easily drop into the air and fly away when disturbed.

Bat

Size: 3 to 4 inches long
(wingspan 6 to 14 inches wide); 1 to 3 ounces.

IDENTIFICATION & GENERAL INFORMATION

Most bats are chocolate brown in color. In college, I had to catch bats as part of a research project and was surprised to discover that they weigh only 1 to 3 ounces.

What people fear most about bats is the possibility of contracting rabies, but the odds of that are actually very low. The bigger concern should be histoplasmosis, a fungal disease found in bat droppings that can cause lung problems in people and pets.

PREVENTATIVE & LOW-IMPACT TREATMENT

They key is prevention. If bats begin to roost in your attic, immediately start building them out. A plastic bird netting works well. Should a bat get into the main living area of your home, put on thick gloves and go after it with a fishing net. Another option is to call upon your county's animal control department. Putting bat houses at the rear of your property is a good idea in bat country.

CHEMICAL TREATMENT

None

BEDBUGS

Your mother may have told you to not let the bedbugs bite, but these bloodsucking insects still haven't gotten the message. They hide in cracks and crevices during the day, waiting to come out at night and feed on warm bodies. Their favorite hiding places are bed frames, mattresses or other furniture. While bedbugs are not classified as disease-carriers, they nonetheless are a major source of irritation and can be a very legitimate cause of insomnia.

When bedbugs bite, the result is often a hard, whitish swelling. This distinguishes it from a flea bite, which leaves a dark red spot surrounded by a reddened area. But take heart all you bedbug bite sufferers, some people gain immunity to the little critters' poison after a while.

Although once associated only with squalid domestic conditions and poor hygienic surroundings, bedbugs actually thrive anywhere they find themselves. While never washing your bedding will provide a nice harborage for bedbugs, even well-maintained homes suffer the effects of these bloodsucking pests.

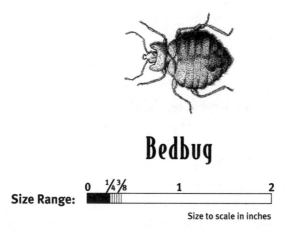

Bedbug

Size Range:

0 ¼ ⅜ 1 2

Size to scale in inches

IDENTIFICATION & GENERAL INFORMATION

This small, brownish and wingless insect depends on a blood meal to survive, but is not a common household pest. The size of the bedbug expands and its color becomes darker after it has fed.

PREVENTATIVE & LOW-IMPACT TREATMENT

Because bedbugs can't fly, they must either crawl inside your home, or be transported in clothing, luggage, furniture, books or other means of entry. If possible, after you've traveled or bought something at an outdoor flea market, check the purchase for signs of infestation. This is especially true if you've bought a used mattress from someone.

Making it even more difficult to keep these critters away is their ability to go many months without feeding. Because of this, they can be dormant for a while in a used copy of *Dracula*, only to scurry out and suck your blood at night. Once they're inside, however, they stay close to where their hosts sleep. If you're being bitten by bedbugs, inspect your bed frame, mattress, furniture or any crack and crevice near your bed where the critters could be hiding. Discard the infested item, or wash it thoroughly to get rid of the bedbugs.

CHEMICAL TREATMENT

To properly control this pest chemically, I advise you to contact a professional exterminator. If, however, you're determined to take the situation into your own hands, use a pyrethrum-based aerosol sprayed lightly around the back of the headboard, or the cracks and crevices of the bed frame and legs. Do not spray mattresses, pillows, or linens. Though it usually requires several applications, this method may prove effective over time.

Silica aerogel dust applied to likely harborages is also an adequate control measure. Put some of this dust in all the little cracks and crevices around your house where you feel the pests may be populating. You can find this dust under the trade name of Drione. Remember to follow all instructions carefully.

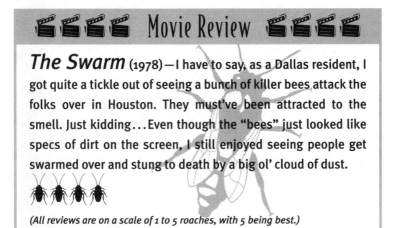

⬛⬛⬛⬛ Movie Review ⬛⬛⬛⬛

The Swarm (1978) — I have to say, as a Dallas resident, I got quite a tickle out of seeing a bunch of killer bees attack the folks over in Houston. They must've been attracted to the smell. Just kidding...Even though the "bees" just looked like specs of dirt on the screen, I still enjoyed seeing people get swarmed over and stung to death by a big ol' cloud of dust.

(All reviews are on a scale of 1 to 5 roaches, with 5 being best.)

BEES, HORNETS, AND WASPS

While some bees can be extremely social, most people would prefer they stick to themselves. Many bees are actually solitary insects that dig deep tunnels while building their nests, boring into banks of earth.

It may be comforting to know that there are about 250 species of stingless bees, although they can still inflict minor irritations. The stingless variety are very small, measuring between 1/16 inch long and about 1/2 inch long.

The hornet, a name given to any social wasp in the family *Vespidae*, inflicts a powerful sting. The name hornet technically applies only to *Vespa crabro*, which first appeared in the United States around 1850. Its nest of grayish paper can typically be found in the hollows of trees, in crevices of rocks or in holes in the foundation of your home. They live in communities comprised of males, females and sterile workers.

Solitary wasps, including the mud dauber, produce no workers and construct individual nests. The females' and worker wasps' stingers are used to attack their prey or to protect the insects against attackers. The sting can be fatal to an especially sensitive person.

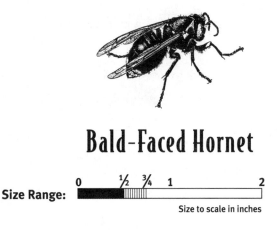

Bald-Faced Hornet

Size Range:

| 0 | ½ | ¾ | 1 | | 2 |

Size to scale in inches

IDENTIFICATION & GENERAL INFORMATION

These are mostly black in color. Depending on the species, however, they will have white or yellowish markings on the abdomen and front of the head. Bald-faced hornets are social insects, and a typical nest contains hundreds of hornets. Be careful when attempting any control measures; they are active stingers. Nests will be found up in trees or hidden in the ground. Guards are posted at the nest opening, which I unfortunately learned the hard way. Two guards got inside my overalls once and repeatedly stung me. And then they had the nerve to wait a whole week before calling again!

PREVENTATIVE & LOW-IMPACT TREATMENT

There's not much you can do to prevent hornets from coming onto your property. If they find a good location, they will let you know. Treatment starts once you notice activity.

Be very cautious around nests. Never cast a shadow on them, keep out of insect flight paths and don't disturb the hornets by making loud noises, thumping the host tree or teasing them with puppets or difficult trivia.

CHEMICAL TREATMENT

Aerial nests should be treated at night or in the cool hours of the morning, before the sun comes up. Always wear protective clothing and exercise extreme caution. Large nests should be handled by a professional pest control operator. I would use two or three cans of a good pressurized hornet and wasp eradicator (the Enforcer brand—active ingredient: tetramethrin—is recommended) that will spray from up to 15 feet away. The key to successful treatment is getting as much of the product as possible inside the nest. The chemical works fast; when hit, the hornets drop like flies.

For ground nests, use an approved insecticide dust. Treat the entrance with a hand-bulb duster, and try to get as much down the opening as possible. You can also use an aerosol pyrethrum.

Be careful—several guards will be posted at the entrance. Kill these with a hornet or wasp spray, then proceed with the dusting. Treat only at night and wear protective clothing. Also, do not wear any cologne or perfume while doing this work.

If you see honey bees "dancing" on their comb, it means that they are telling their friends where to find food. The sound and the scent the bees make indicates what's on the menu. A well-choreographed round dance means the food is within 80 meters. The length of the dance—known as a "waggle"—tells the richness of the food source. The angle between the straight and vertical runs shows the bees where the food source is in relation to the sun. The angle of the dance changes as the sun moves across the sky.

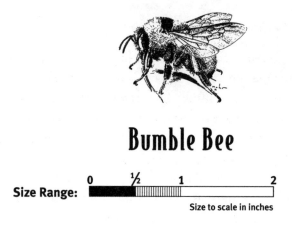

Bumble Bee

Size Range:

0   ½   1   2

Size to scale in inches

IDENTIFICATION & GENERAL INFORMATION

This large, black-colored bee has patches of yellow hair. It likes to build its nest near the ground, often in piles of grass clippings, under woodpiles, or under children's playhouses. Note: bees pollinate flowers and are very useful. Unless it is absolutely necessary, do not disturb them.

PREVENTATIVE & LOW-IMPACT TREATMENT

Remove any potential harborages in your yard like heaps of old wood or garden trimmings. Because bumble bees like low-lying nests, concentrate especially on areas close to the ground that may attract these insects. If you have a hollow tree or trees in your yard that may provide a nice nesting space, remove the plant or plug the opening if possible.

Try to avoid planting flowering plants close to your home that may attract pollen-hungry bumble bees. Taking away incentives for stinging insects to hang out around your house is a good way to ensure that they pose no risk to your family or pets.

CHEMICAL TREATMENT

Once the nest site is found, return at night with a flashlight and treat it with an approved product. Use a liquid insecticide, mixed with one to two gallons of water. Water will carry the mixture down to the core of the nest. Night work is necessary because all the bees will be back in the nest and your chances of getting stung are lessened. Don't hold the flashlight during treatment—instead place it on the ground, at an angle away from you.

Alternatively, with a hand-bulb duster, use a product that contains silica aerogel (Drione). Put a liberal amount of dust inside the entrance of the nest. Do the work at night, following the procedure outlined above. The next day, apply another treatment and seal the hole entrance with dirt.

Most of a queen bee's subjects are workers who are too busy to breed. To fill a honeycomb cell, a worker bee visits up to one thousand succulent flowers. To make just two pounds of honey, bees must make up to 65 thousand trips—landing on 45 million to 65 million flowers. There are nearly 80 thousand workers in large bee colonies. Worker bees live just six to eight weeks, while the queen can live up to five years.

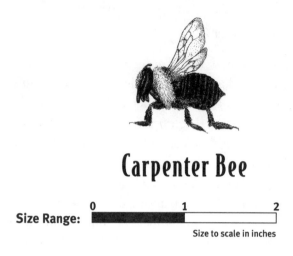

Carpenter Bee

Size Range:

| 0 | 1 | 2 |

Size to scale in inches

IDENTIFICATION & GENERAL INFORMATION

This large bee looks very much like a bumble bee, but has more of a metallic shine to its body and no yellow hair on its abdomen. Carpenter bees are seen only in the warmest part of summer, when they make their nests. The entrance to the nest, measuring about the size of a dime, will often be found on the underside of a wooden patio cover. This bee especially likes to build nests on old cedar.

PREVENTATIVE & LOW-IMPACT TREATMENT

Keep a close eye on outdoor furniture, fences and other wood products for signs of this bee's distinctive nest tunnels. If possible, dispose of the infested item very carefully, or use a chemical treatment described below. To keep the situation from reaching a crisis point, remove potential harborages like unused wooden furniture, play items or piles of loose wood.

Carpenter bees also damage siding, window sills and eaves with their tunneling. Watch for these solitary bees buzzing around these sites, then look closely for signs of nesting.

CHEMICAL TREATMENT

Since the nest is inside the wood, this is where you should apply the chemical. I like to use a residual chemical in an aerosol can with a six to eight inch applicator tip, similar to what is found on a WD-40 can. Treatment is best done at night. Be sure to wear rubber gloves and eye protection. Insert the tube about one inch up inside the nest, then find both tunnels—the one that goes to the right and the one that goes to the left—and spray the chemical into each. Wait one day, then plug the holes with caulking material.

Cicada Killer

Size: 1 1/2 to 2 1/2 inches long.

IDENTIFICATION & GENERAL INFORMATION

This extremely large wasp is brownish-black in color, with yellow stripes on the abdomen. Its name refers to—no surprise—its practice of hunting cicadas, then carrying them to burrows as food for their young.

In the summer months, the female will search for a sandy or soft dirt area to dig out her nest. The entrance will be about 3/4 inch wide, with a pile of loose dirt at the base. This is not an aggressive wasp, unless you step on the nest. Normally, this wasp is only visible to us during one season of the year—the summer. You will find most nests near swimming pools or gardens.

PREVENTATIVE & LOW-IMPACT TREATMENT

Watch your lawn or the dirt areas in your yard for this wasp's distinctive nest. If you can identify a potential infestation early, you may be able to disturb the wasp enough that it seeks a safer burrow for its young.

In general, however, this insect will not attack humans, and even controls a potentially bothersome garden pest. Only eradicate cicada killers if you feel they have become an uncontrollable nuisance. They are nature's cicada exterminator.

CHEMICAL TREATMENT

Forget the hornet and wasp spray—it won't penetrate down inside the nest. At night or very early in the morning, carefully approach the nest and spray an insecticide down the hole and about six inches around the entrance. Then push the loose dirt into the hole and spray the area again.

You can also use a dust like silica aerogel (Drione) and treat each entrance to the nest. After treatment, push the expelled dirt inside the hole and step on it. When treating nests in the garden, be careful what you use; you don't want to contaminate the garden. Use only approved products.

Your neighbors may be loud, but the male cicada is louder. Its mating sound can be heard as far as 440 yards away—longer than four football fields. The cicada makes noise by vibrating the ribbed plates in a pair of amplifying cavities at the base of its abdomen.

Honey Bee

Size Range:

0 ¼ ½ 1 2

Size to scale in inches

IDENTIFICATION & GENERAL INFORMATION

This yellowish-brown bee lives in large colonies, some of which house between 20,000 and 80,000 insects. Most of the time, this species is non-aggressive and situates its nests in tree cavities or holes leading to the outside walls of homes. If left undisturbed, the honey bee will use the same nest year after year. This bee, which produces both honey and beeswax, is economically the most valuable of all insects. It is a social creature that can survive only as a member of a community. If you really want to kill this bee, you've obviously never had honey on your English muffins.

PREVENTATIVE & LOW-IMPACT TREATMENT

If you plant the bright, succulent flowers that attract these bees a good distance from your home or children's play area, they shouldn't bother you. Honey bees aren't looking to sting humans, and will only attack if provoked. While they can become pests by nesting in wall voids, if you ensure that potential exterior entry points are sealed securely, this won't be a problem.

If you do find a colony of honey bees in a location you deem dangerous to your family's welfare, try to contact a local beekeeper to remove the nest for you. Bees are very useful in nature and should not be killed unless they enter the walls of your home and start stinging everyone.

CHEMICAL TREATMENT

Nests inside wall voids should be eradicated to lessen the chance of people being stung. Most of the time, the entry point is in a secluded area of the home. A crack in a brick or a hole in the mortar around a window are ideal nest sites. When all of the bees are in the nest, dust the entrance with a bulb duster and a residual dust. Tip: cover yourself with protective gear and use a flashlight for improved vision.

Gas the wall void with a labeled aerosol insecticide and a crack-and-crevice applicator (pyrethrum works the best). The gassing should reach the queen, located deep in the nest. If you put your ear to the wall, most of the time you should hear buzzing. The buzzing should stop and bees eradicated by the next day.

Don't plug the nest hole until a week later. If the honey bees have been in the wall for a long time, consider removing the nest by opening the wall and throwing away the comb and honey. If you leave the comb and honey in the wall, they will likely attract other pests such as moths, carpet beetles and other bee colonies.

Forget about using a hornet or wasp spray for eradication. These products will only get rid of the insects at the entrance of the nest.

Alternatively, you could use a dust like Drione or Delta-Dust. Follow all label instructions carefully.

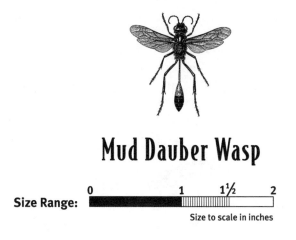

Mud Dauber Wasp

Size Range:

0   1   1½   2

Size to scale in inches

IDENTIFICATION & GENERAL INFORMATION

This medium-size wasp is mostly black or brown in color, with a few yellow markings. The easiest identification marker is the narrow area between its thorax and abdomen. This wasp feeds on spiders, is solitary and does not nest in groups. Mud daubers are not very aggressive and most likely will not bother you. Their nests are made of mud and are found on the outside walls of the home, in attics or storage sheds.

PREVENTATIVE & LOW-IMPACT TREATMENT

Keep an eye on your home's walls, attic or storage shed for signs of wasp activity. If you do find a mud dauber nest, it is one of the easiest to eradicate. With only one occupant—the egg-laying female—this nest can be easily destroyed with a long pole. When the one wasp is either just entering or leaving the nest, smack her with a fly swatter. If you don't want to kill the insect, trap it in a jar and set it loose somewhere far away from your home. This method may lead to you getting stung, but I guess the good karma's worth it.

CHEMICAL TREATMENT

Should you have some adult mud daubers flying around inside your home, use an aerosol spray that contains pyrethrins. Sometimes, fogging the attic is needed if the population level is high.

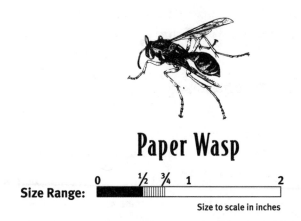

Paper Wasp

Size Range:
0   ½ ¾ 1   2

Size to scale in inches

IDENTIFICATION & GENERAL INFORMATION

These reddish-orange, dark brown, or black-colored wasps like to build paper umbrella-shaped nests in the eaves of homes, attics or in storage sheds. They are extremely social and can be dangerous when they nest near doors and windows. This is the most common wasp found across the United States.

PREVENTATIVE & LOW-IMPACT TREATMENT

Seal any crevices in the exterior of your home, as well as any holes in screens that may allow the wasps to build nests in wall voids, eaves or attics.

During the warmer months when these wasps scavenge, make sure to keep your windows and doors either closed or screened to guarantee that the insects won't have a way into your house.

If you happen to find a paper wasp nest, never just knock it down and expect the problem to go away. The wasps will quickly rebuild their nest, and they probably won't be too happy about it, either. Don't squish a wasp, because a chemical pheromone will be released that will attract other wasps to come and sting you.

CHEMICAL TREATMENT

Treatment should be done at night, when most of the wasps will be around the nest. I recommend the Enforcer brand of insecticide, which can be found at most hardware and variety stores. After treatment, scrape off the nest and throw it away. During chemical application, have someone hold a flashlight away from where you're standing. With this precaution, the wasps will be less likely to see you should they fly off the nest.

You can also use a hornet spray that contains synergized pyrethrins. As always, use caution.

Movie Review

The Wasp Women (1959) — Famed low-budget director Roger Corman offered up this tale of a cosmetics magnate whose search for eternal beauty leads her to take a potion made from wasp enzymes. Then, shock-of-shocks, she turns into a wasp monster at night and goes on big-time stinging and killing sprees. Although this flick is considered a cult favorite, I thought there were some serious shortcomings. First of all, any member of the insect order of hymenoptera is supposed to have antennae much shorter than their body and no noticeable scales. Now, I'm not sure what kind of costume get-up they had this lady in, but she wasn't no wasp. I guess she could've almost passed as a horntail wasp, but I sure as heck didn't see her infesting any lumber.

(All reviews are on a scale of 1 to 5 roaches, with 5 being best.)

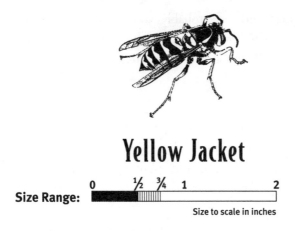

Yellow Jacket

Size Range:

| 0 | ½ | ¾ | 1 | | 2 |

Size to scale in inches

IDENTIFICATION & GENERAL INFORMATION

This small to medium-sized species of social wasp features some very unpredictable workers. Sometimes they'll sting you, sometimes they won't. But it's not smart to test your luck, all things considered. Black in color with yellow stripes, yellow jackets are very aggressive and should be not be incited in any way, regardless of the frequency of their attacks.

They make both aerial and ground nests, and protect each with the war-like enthusiasm of other wasp species. If you're at all allergic to any type of sting, I'd recommend calling out a professional to handle a yellow jacket infestation.

PREVENTATIVE & LOW-IMPACT TREATMENT

Since yellow jackets' underground nests are usually started in an abandoned animal burrow, or other available ground-level opening, try to ensure that no gopher holes or other mammal burrows are exposed. Covering openings in concrete block foundations, or below landscaped railroad ties, will also help discourage nest building.

This pest's tendency to scavenge human food sources puts yellow jackets in repeated conflict with people in backyard patios, parks and picnic areas. Keep sugary foods and beverages tightly sealed or covered to avoid attracting yellow jackets looking for sweets and honeydew for their new queens.

Chemical Treatment

For the aerial nests, wait until it's dark, then use the Enforcer brand insecticide to knock down the guards. When they're out of the way, proceed with the heavy spray into the core of the nest. Be careful that the chemical doesn't fall back into your face. Wearing safety goggles and the proper clothing is a must when tackling this job.

A good residual dust will work well on the ground nests. Again, wait until nightfall, then use a medium-sized bulb duster to blast the product into the core of the nest. In a short time, the adults and larvae should be dead.

The threat of getting bitten isn't the only reason not to squash a yellow jacket near its nest. A dying yellow jacket releases an alarm pheromone that alerts nearby wasps. When that happens, yellow jackets within 15-foot radius will immediately rally around.

BEETLES

With over 200,000 varieties of beetle—25,000 in North America alone—this insect comprises the largest major group in the animal kingdom. By sheer numbers alone, adult beetles can become a gardener's worst enemy, munching on flowers and leaves until there are only bare skeletons remaining of once vital foliage. When they feed on and destroy the roots, wood, leaves, flowers and fruit of living plants, beetles can cause serious damage.

Beetles can even be unwelcome guests in the homes of other insects, moving into the nests of bees, termites or ants. They've been known to eat the food brought in by their hosts, and even devour the hosts themselves. How's that for hospitality?

The carpet beetle, which has an appetite for rugs and fabrics, can even inflict more damage than the notorious clothes moth. Fur, leather, and wool clothing that has been stored for an extended period doesn't stand a chance against an onslaught of hungry beetles.

Their diverse habitats, including salt water, fresh water and even hot springs, truly make beetles the Robin Leaches of household pests, traveling the world over in search of the finest things to sink their freeloading teeth into.

One of every five living species is a beetle.

Black Carpet Beetle

Size Range: 0 ⅛ ¼   1   2

Size to scale in inches

IDENTIFICATION & GENERAL INFORMATION

This beetle is shiny black in color and somewhat oval in shape. While the adults are pollen feeders, it is the larvae that cause the serious damage. They are fond of woolen clothes and will chew holes in your favorite stored garments. Most damage to woolen clothes is found in the fall when these items are removed from storage. Larvae look like brown "Rice Krispies" and can be found in corners of closets or pantries. The adults are attracted to light and usually cluster around window sills.

PREVENTATIVE & LOW-IMPACT TREATMENT

After you positively identify this bug, then you need to find the source of the infestation. If you think they've been attacking particular food products, throw those items away and vacuum any larvae or adults you see. Clothes that are infested should be taken to a dry cleaner.

Sanitation is the key. Vacuum under furniture and in closets on a regular basis. Try to seal all cracks and crevices on the outside of your home, as well as holes in door and window screens. This will help to build out the adults. Bird nests in attics may have to be removed since they also attract the black carpet beetle.

CHEMICAL TREATMENT

The use of an insecticide should be limited to spot applications in cracks and crevices of baseboards. Follow all label guidelines for specific usages. Use a residual type product. Don't fog the closet; it will ruin your clothes.

Don't provoke a bombardier beetle. It will swivel the top of its abdomen and shoot a jet of boiling chemicals at its attacker. The chemicals are brewed in a "reaction chamber" that produces a loud explosion. The spray of the foul-smelling, burning vapor is the result of rapid firing. It shoots out at up to one thousand pulses a second at a temperature of one hundred degrees Celsius.

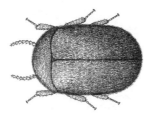

Cigarette Beetle

Size: 1/16 to 1/8 inch long.

IDENTIFICATION & GENERAL INFORMATION

This reddish-brown beetle looks like a hunchback. Under low magnification, you can see the insect's head bending in a downward position, creating the shape of a hump. As the name implies, it will infest tobacco products as well as spices, seeds, nuts and dried fruits. Because of their small size, they can enter any type of package. The largest infestation I have ever seen was in my own home—in paprika that we hadn't used for years. When I told my wife to "spice up" dinner that night, adding a pack of cigarette beetles really wasn't what I had in mind. In addition to being excellent flyers, these beetles are also attracted to light, so they'll often be found at the window, away from the infested area.

PREVENTATIVE & LOW-IMPACT TREATMENT

Find the infested products and throw them out. Empty all your kitchen cupboards and wash the shelves with warm, soapy water. Vacuum up any adults and larvae, and carefully inspect all stored food products, even unopened boxes. You should also rotate food supplies and buy your staples in moderate amounts. The more food you have on hand, and the longer you keep it, the higher the risk of infestation. Christmas dough ornaments are also potential problem items.

Also, don't leave dog food sitting around in the dish for hours at a time. Pooch chow is one of this beetle's favorite meals, and it will rarely turn down what your dog couldn't finish.

CHEMICAL TREATMENT

None. You should not use chemicals in food storage areas.

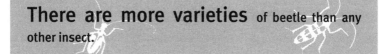

There are more varieties of beetle than any other insect.

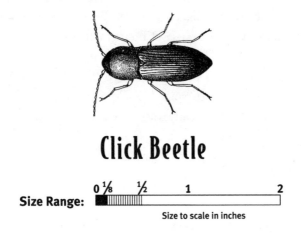

Click Beetle

Size Range:

0 ⅛   ½   1   2

Size to scale in inches

IDENTIFICATION & GENERAL INFORMATION

This small beetle ranges in color from dark brown to dark gray. When found inside the home, they will usually be at the base of lamps or on window sills. The larvae are called wireworms and live in the ground, while the adults are attracted to bright light at building entrances. The insect makes a very distinctive clicking sound, which makes them much in demand for beetle bands.

PREVENTATIVE & LOW-IMPACT TREATMENT

Remove any decaying tree stumps or old fire logs from your yard that may provide harborage for beetle larvae. Also, since many adult click beetle species are attracted to light, illumination from lamps or naked bulbs may attract these critters to your doorway or window. Then, when you go to let in a little fresh air, some click beetles hoof in without you even knowing.

Installation of yellow bug lights, and repair of damaged seals at all entry points will most likely keep these pests on the outside looking in. For the very few that do get inside, simply grab a tissue paper and pick them up (they don't bite), and deposit them outside. Alternatively, you can add them to your bug collection!

CHEMICAL TREATMENT

Establish a barrier on the outside of your home, stopping most of these beetles before they can get inside. Spray a residual chemical along the lower portion of the foundation and, if needed, dust a residual-type granule in the ground area next to the house. Make sure to pour water over the granules so that they will soak into the soil. Once they cross the barrier treatment, most click beetles will perish within a few feet so there is no need to treat the inside of the house.

Pests that infest stored foods in our homes create major economic losses worldwide, damaging as much as 50 percent of food products in some developing countries.

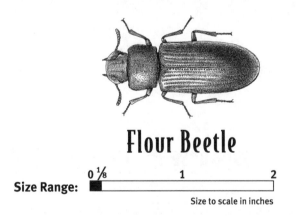

Flour Beetle

Size Range: 0 ⅛   1   2

Size to scale in inches

IDENTIFICATION & GENERAL INFORMATION

This reddish-brown, slim beetle has a "sweet tooth" and likes to feed on chocolate. And because their mouths are so large, they can consume whole grains at a time, in addition to flour, dust, nuts and spices. This is one of the most common beetles to infest the pantry.

There are two types of flour beetle, the red flour beetle and the confused flour beetle, and their appearance is similar. The main difference is that the latter has never been able to understand Daylight Savings Time.

PREVENTATIVE & LOW-IMPACT TREATMENT

Forget using sprays; sanitation and the removal of the infested products will solve the problem. Empty the pantry, wash all shelves with warm soapy water, and vacuum up any adults or larvae. As you return items to the shelves, open all packages and throw away those that contain bugs.

CHEMICAL TREATMENT

None

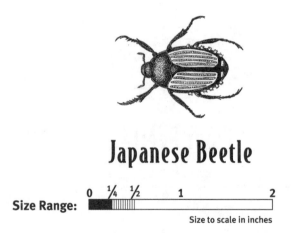

Japanese Beetle

Size Range:
0   ¼   ½   1   2

Size to scale in inches

IDENTIFICATION & GENERAL INFORMATION

Bronze wing covers and a metallic green body rimmed by tufts of white hair make this beetle a real looker. They will be easy to spot as they're most active on warm, sunny days when their bodies positively glimmer. The grubs are white, C-shaped insects with brown heads. Adults feed on the leaves of various shrubs and plants, while the grubs munch on decaying vegetation and roots.

Because Japanese beetles are most active in the warmer months, look for warning signs in early spring like irregular patches of dying, yellowing grass. The infested areas should roll back easily to the touch because their roots have been eaten away by the grubs.

PREVENTATIVE & LOW-IMPACT TREATMENT

Because the adults lay eggs in moist soil, and the eggs need wetness to hatch, try not to keep your lawn and garden drenched during the late spring and summer. Deep, but infrequent irrigations will keep your plants healthy, but minimize the amount of time the soil is damp.

As mentioned above, these beetles are day feeders, and are pretty easy to handpick because of their eye-catching color and their early-morning sluggishness. After you pluck them, drop the beetles in a bucket of soapy water to kill them.

A longer-term control is the introduction of milky spore disease into your lawn. You can buy the disease spores in powder form at your local garden store, but be sure to wear a mask when applying it. Then lightly water your lawn to wash the spores into the soil. It may take a season or two before the disease has a significant impact on grub populations.

You also may want to try planting some geranium or garlic in your garden. Japanese beetles will hightail and scurry if they sense the stuff is near.

CHEMICAL TREATMENT

A chemical called neem oil can be sprayed on leaves will protect them from Japanese beetles. The bugs would rather starve than eat neem-covered foliage. Pyrethrum or pyrethroid-based products are also effective when sprayed on adults. As always, use these products safely and sparingly so you don't kill the predator bugs along with the pests.

> **Scarab beetles** were used on jewelry in Ancient Egypt because of the beautiful colors of the adult insect.

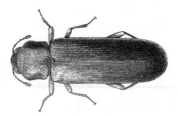

Powder Post Beetle

Size: 1/16 to 1/8 inch long.

IDENTIFICATION & GENERAL INFORMATION

This very small beetle is black or dark brown in color. Interestingly, the beetle itself is usually never seen. Rather, people usually find the holes it makes in wood. Most infestations are found in hardwoods, but some softwoods are also susceptible. The holes are about the size of a pinhead, and below them will be a fine powder known as frass. During the home construction boom in the 1980s, much of the hardwood used for trim was not properly cured; as a result, pests have emerged. They can stay inside the wood for years and will emerge only when the conditions are right. Like when there's something really good on TV.

PREVENTATIVE & LOW-IMPACT TREATMENT

Keep an eye on all wood surfaces in your home, and check for powder post beetle infestation regularly. Also, if you see some of the frass around wood-heavy areas, you likely have a problem.

If the infestation is minor, the damaged wood should be replaced. If not, see below.

CHEMICAL TREATMENT

If the infestation has penetrated the entire house, fumigation may be needed. Complete tarping of the house may be required and the cost will be high. This is definitely a job for a professional; do-it-yourselfers should not attempt it. Get the yellow pages out and "let your fingers do the walking."

The majority of pantry pests originated in the tropics and subtropics and have been spread throughout the world in infested products.

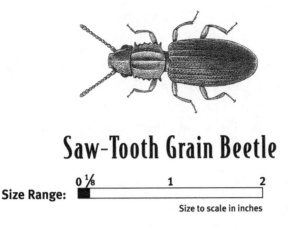

Saw-Tooth Grain Beetle

Size Range:

```
0 ⅛        1           2
```

Size to scale in inches

IDENTIFICATION & GENERAL INFORMATION

This slim, reddish-brown beetle is easy to identify by the six-pointed projections on each side of its thorax. It's not a good flyer and will be found close to the infested product. Saw-tooth beetles are attracted to items such as flour, cereals, dried fruit and sugar. Because they're flat-shaped, the insect has an easy time getting inside unopened boxes of food.

Temperatures above 80 degrees Fahrenheit trigger the hatching of this pest, so take care not to let your kitchen stay very hot for extended periods of time.

PREVENTATIVE & LOW-IMPACT TREATMENT

Once you get rid of the infestation source, the problem will disappear. As with other pantry pests, wash all shelves with soapy warm water and vacuum up any adults and larvae. As you put items back on shelves, look into each box—even unopened boxes—and throw away products that contain bugs. Also, keep the temperature of your food-storage areas down to a manageable level.

CHEMICAL TREATMENT

None

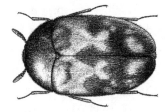

Varied Carpet Beetle

Size: 1/16 to 1/8 inch long.

IDENTIFICATION & GENERAL INFORMATION

The adult beetle has a mixture of tan, white and brown scales on the topside of its body. Much like its cousin, the black carpet beetle, the adults of this species leave the real mayhem to the kids. The damage caused by the small, black carpet beetle larvae is a byproduct of the bugs' appetite for the keratin found in all hair and hair-derived products like wool, mink, and cashmere.

In an infested area, you will find larval skins stuck to the corners of drawers or closets. Sometimes even cotton will be attacked if it is soiled. Of the three types of insects that infest clothes, the varied carpet beetle is the most common.

PREVENTATIVE & LOW-IMPACT TREATMENT

Take everything out of your closet, then do a thorough sanitation and vacuuming job. Many times you can suck up the larvae as they crawl on the wall. Inspect all your clothes as you return them to the closet, and set aside any suspect garments for dry-cleaning.

CHEMICAL TREATMENT

The first thing you should do is inspect your closet to locate the heaviest area of infestation. Use an approved pyrethrum or a pyrethroid such as permethrin to spray in cracks and crevices, where walls meet and in the grooves at the back of all shelf areas. You don't need to spray the entire house, just those areas where woolens are stored. Never use foggers to combat this beetle as they can do more damage to clothes than the bugs themselves.

You may need to use a residual spray (synthetic pyrethroid) to obtain lasting control, but make sure it's a spot application. Follow label recommendations and never use the spray on your clothes. It's for the baseboard and crack and crevice areas only.

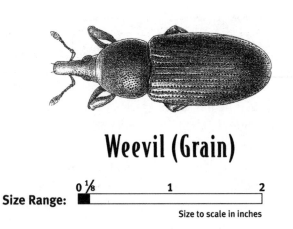

Weevil (Grain)

Size Range: 0 ⅛   1   2

Size to scale in inches

IDENTIFICATION & GENERAL INFORMATION

This beetle is easily identified by its long snout and elbowed antennae. Weevils vary in color from jet black to reddish brown. Of all the food products that whet their whistles, they like wheat, corn, rice and dry dog or cat food the best.

PREVENTATIVE & LOW-IMPACT TREATMENT

Treatment is similar to that of the other pantry beetles. No spraying is needed, but you must remove all products from food-storage areas and wash the shelves with warm soapy water. Should you spot any weevils walking around, suck them up with the vacuum. As you put items back on the shelves, inspect packages and throw away all that show signs of infestation. In the future, rotate packages on the shelves or keep some bulk products in the freezer.

CHEMICAL TREATMENT

None

Great quantities of pantry pests can breed within food products. A bag of grain, for example, can contain more than 40 thousand grain weevils.

BIRDS

Even before Alfred Hitchcock decided to feature winged creatures snacking on human carcasses in *The Birds*, experts have known that certain species can be harmful to your health.

A few pigeons in a park may seem pleasant, but they can be a source of many public health problems. Their droppings on benches, water fountains, and the unlucky pedestrian's new sports coat are known to carry a large number of diseases, including salmonella. Pigeons are also known to carry fleas, ticks and mites. Nearly all pigeons in a flock can be infected without visible effects.

Even the seemingly innocent house sparrow is not as benign as you may think. Measuring about six inches in length, the sparrow was brought to the United States in the 19th century with the hope it would control the insect population. The plan backfired as the little bird became a big pest, devouring huge amounts of grain and vegetable crops. It isn't a very good housekeeper, either. Its messy nest of coarse grass lined with feathers is usually built in the crannies of buildings, and can be a serious eyesore.

The brain of a pigeon is only four grams in weight. So next time someone calls you a "pigeon brain," go ahead and smack 'em!

Pigeon

Size: 10 to 12 inches long.

IDENTIFICATION & GENERAL INFORMATION

Most pigeons are gray in color, with a whitish band on their breast
and two black bars on their wings. Their legs are most commonly
red, and their heads shine with a green iridescence. Large flocks
of pigeons will be found wherever food, or tourists, are abundant.
The droppings of pigeons contain bacteria fungal agents and
ectoparasites, as well as uric acid—a highly corrosive agent that
can damage fabric, metal and car paint.

PREVENTATIVE & LOW-IMPACT TREATMENT

Visual distractions such as scarecrows, plastic owls or hawks, and
balloons are moderately effective. However, the two main pigeon-
control methods are repellents and trapping. If you take the time to
pre-bait the area that pigeons are invading, they can be caught fairly easily. Special pigeon traps can catch up to 12 birds at a time.

You can repel the birds from the ledges they're roosting on by
using a "sticky gel," applied with a caulking gun. Stainless steel or
plastic "porcupine"-type projections secured to the ledges are also
effective for preventing the birds from landing. Sound machines,

which I have not used, emit the stress sound of the pigeon and would seem like a good idea, too. I also recommend a product that is relatively new to the market called Bird-Coil, essentially a rolled wire that looks like a Slinky.

CHEMICAL TREATMENT

None

Pigeons were domesticated by the Romans.

Sparrow

Size: 4 to 5 inches long.

IDENTIFICATION & GENERAL INFORMATION

This small brown and grayish bird is fun to watch at a feeder, but not when it destroys your car's finish with its droppings. Equally unpleasant is when it nests near your home and defaces the exterior.

Sparrows are prolific, having four to five families a year. As you may expect, scientists are still perfecting the "sparrow condom." With so many of them around, this bird naturally congregates in flocks. Being grain-lovers, they will hang out at just about any bird feeder in the neighborhood.

PREVENTATIVE & LOW-IMPACT TREATMENT

Mechanical controls include a number of "porcupine"-type prong products currently available. Some are stainless steel, others are plastic.

For small populations of sparrows, trapping is easy. Traps are available that will catch many of these birds at one time. I have used the Tomahawk brand, model 50, with great success.

If your budget allows it, there are also companies that will install low-voltage electrical wires to prevent sparrow roosting. Sticky gels are also effective, and they are much cheaper. They are applied with a caulking gun, and one tube covers about ten linear feet. The best sticky gel I have used is made by Eaton's and is called 4 the Birds.

CHEMICAL TREATMENT

A number of poison grains are on the market, but I would not recommend them. These grains are only available to certified applicators and special precautions must be followed when using them.

Starling

Size: 5 to 7 inches long.

IDENTIFICATION & GENERAL INFORMATION

This black-colored bird is easy to identify by the speckled pattern on its feathers, which produces a greenish or purplish iridescence. The beak is normally bright yellow. While generally a benign bird, their droppings nonetheless create quite a mess. Also, their constant warbling is annoying to some. They tend to sing the same song over and over again like a broken record.

PREVENTATIVE & LOW-IMPACT TREATMENT

Try to discourage them from nesting on your property. Use expanding foam or copper mesh to plug all holes leading into your attic.

Anti-roost material is another good way to prevent these birds from nesting in your attic or under your eaves. These products can be purchased at most home-and-garden centers and are essentially multi-pronged attachments that you fasten to a wooden surface with nails or screws. Picture a spaghetti spoon lashed onto a roof beam in your attic. A bird trying to make a nest on this thing will get poked and jabbed a couple times, then go looking for a less difficult residence.

Sticky gels on ledges also work well. They are applied with a caulking gun, and one tube covers about ten linear feet. I usually recommend a sticky gel made by Eaton's called 4 the Birds.

Forget using traps to catch starlings; they usually won't enter them.

CHEMICAL TREATMENT

None

CATERPILLARS, CENTIPEDES, AND MILLIPEDES

The caterpillar is a big-time eater, taking in more than its own weight in food each day. But few reach maturity, instead falling victim to hungry birds, reptiles and even harsh weather. But as any gardener knows, the caterpillar does a lot of damage in a little time, wreaking havoc on plants and the green portions of trees. If they do escape harm, they will eventually become any one of thousands of species of butterflies and moths. Only a relatively few of these flying insects become significant pests.

The word millipede may mean thousand-footed, but this worm-like insect actually has far fewer legs than you'd think. With anywhere from 15 to 150 body segments, each with two pairs of legs, the millipede will usually have a maximum of only 300 legs. Even with all of that leg power, it is surprisingly slow moving.

The millipede crawls into homes during the fall season, then again during spring, forced indoors when heavy rains raise the water level of soil. They are short-term pests, but arrive by the hundreds. Think Thanksgiving dinner with the relatives.

Because it has too many legs, the centipede is not technically considered an insect. The average adult house centipede has 15 to 30 pairs of extremely long legs and a body divided into well-marked rings. Interestingly, many varieties of the centipede do not have eyes. Instead, their feelers, bristles and portions of the skin give them sensory perception.

The centipede moves at the amazing speed of nearly 25 miles an hour.

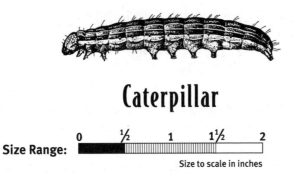

Caterpillar

Size Range:

0	½	1	1½	2

Size to scale in inches

IDENTIFICATION & GENERAL INFORMATION

Body color is usually greenish, allowing the crawler to blend in well with leaves and foliage. Caterpillars are actually the larvae of butterflies and moths. They begin as eggs, shed their skin a number of times as larvae and then rest in a pupal stage until an adult moth or butterfly emerges. Larvae are either exposed or hidden. The exposed variety feeds in the open, then hides, while the hidden type either burrows into a plant or fruit to feed, or fashions its own shelter from rolled-up leaves. The exposed caterpillars are much easier to locate and eliminate.

PREVENTATIVE & LOW-IMPACT TREATMENT

Sometimes, the simplest treatment is plucking the little suckers off the leaves they're eating. Or you can diversify your ground cover with plants such as clover or mulch to increase populations of predatory ground beetles and toads. Also, as stated before, caterpillars are quite tasty to a number of airborne and ground-based attackers, so you often won't even have to worry about them.

CHEMICAL TREATMENT

The most appropriate pesticide is *Bacillus Thuringiensis* (BT). It is sold under several brand names including Caterpillar Killer,

Javelin and Worm Attack. BT is a stomach poison that kills the caterpillar after it has eaten the treated plant material.

A last resort is pyrethrum dust. Apply only to infested plants and only on areas clearly munched on by caterpillars. Never disperse this product around water sources, as it is highly toxic to fish and certain aquatic invertebrates.

 Movie Review

Mothra (1962)—I just love this classic Japanese bug flick. The story starts off with two princesses getting taken from their island home to perform in a Tokyo nightclub. Her pissed off native tribe prays for her return, which causes this giant egg to be made. The egg hatches a giant caterpillar who crawls to Tokyo to look for the princesses. The giant caterpillar wreaks havoc on the city, then pops into a giant chrysalis and emerges as Mothra, the killer moth. The only thing missing is a giant light bulb for Mothra to flap into all the time. All in all, a great, great insect film.

(All reviews are on a scale of 1 to 5 roaches, with 5 being best.)

Centipede

Size: 1 1/2 inches to 12 inches long.

IDENTIFICATION & GENERAL INFORMATION

Body color ranges from brown to black, with orange-colored legs. Be careful: this pest can bite and has poison glands on its head. Each body segment has one pair of legs. Unlike its friend the millipede, the centipede can run very fast and likes to hide under rocks and pieces of wood.

PREVENTATIVE & LOW-IMPACT TREATMENT

Trim all bushes next to the house, creating an air barrier. Remove hiding materials such as rocks, wood and leaves that may be next to the house. Caulk all foundation holes and place copper mesh over any potential entry points to keep most of the pests outside. Glue boards will catch those that get into the house.

CHEMICAL TREATMENT

Most control is done outside the house. Use a micro-encapsulated chemical, and spray the thresholds of all doorways. Also treat the outside walls six inches up and away from the foundation. Most centipedes never make it inside the home, or will be found dead at the doorways.

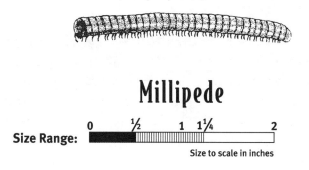

Millipede

Size Range:

| 0 | ½ | 1 | 1¼ | 2 |

Size to scale in inches

IDENTIFICATION & GENERAL INFORMATION

Usually brown colored, this critter can be spotted curling up on its side to sleep. Normally an outside pest, it will venture inside if the seals at the bases of doors are in disrepair. Millipedes don't bite and cause no damage should they get inside the home.

PREVENTATIVE & LOW-IMPACT TREATMENT

Reduce the amount of organic material adjacent to your home. Trim bushes and keep leaves and debris from collecting on the ground outside your house. The use of glue boards inside will catch millipedes that manage sneak past your outside defenses.

CHEMICAL TREATMENT

A liquid or granular insecticide placed along the foundation of your home will do a good job keeping this insect's numbers down. And spraying the thresholds of all doorways will kill most of them before they have a chance to get inside.

FERAL CATS

Feral cats are either born wild, are abandoned or have escaped from homes and never returned. They can carry many diseases and should not be allowed to come in contact with your domestic pets. More times than not, feral cats are not spayed and will either spray or moan incessantly when in heat. It is during these times that they will be most attracted to your pet, or another domestic outdoor cat.

These wild cats can be very dangerous when cornered. Once I caught one live in a humane trap and he literally destroyed it. Feral cats can give birth to many litters in a year, which rapidly increases their population.

Feral Cat

Size: 1 1/2 to 2 1/2 feet long; 8 to 10 pounds.

IDENTIFICATION & GENERAL INFORMATION

Feral cats are indistinguishable from domestic cats on the surface, but if you look closer, you may find some clues. First of all, they'll never have any identification tags of any kind, and will probably be very people-shy, running away from you before you get within five feet of them.

Also, feral cats tend to be mangy-looking, and won't be groomed as meticulously as domestic pet cats. A telltale sign of a wild cat is either spraying to mark territory or moaning when in heat. Most domestic cats are usually spayed and don't get all lathered up when spring comes around.

PREVENTATIVE & LOW-IMPACT TREATMENT

Live trapping is the best approach; it is humane and the success rate is high. Contact your local animal control department, where you may be able to obtain traps. They can also tell you what to do with the cat after you trap it. For bait, I use sardines in oil; the smell of the fish attracts the cat. Tuna also works well. I must stress, proceed with caution at all times. Feral cats can be ferocious. Additionally, before setting a trap for that mangy-looking cat roaming around your backyard, be 100% certain that the animal is truly a wild cat and not your neighbor's beloved kitty. Most local animal control departments have an ideal trap size (26 x 9 x 9 inches), and will pick up these cats for you.

CHEMICAL TREATMENT

None

COCKROACHES

As the most prevalent household pest in the United States, cockroaches can cause severe economic harm and spread disease. Because they thrive in unsanitary places such as sewers and drains, they are like germ magnets, attracting bacteria and bringing it into your home, apartment, trailer, lean-to, shanty or pup tent. Roaches aren't picky as long as there's stuff to eat.

Before we get too crazy hating roaches, I've got a little fact for you that you may find hard to believe: roaches can actually serve a useful purpose. Researchers have utilized them in medical investigations of heart disease, cancer, and even the effects of space travel. It turns out the roach's internal architecture is a reasonable facsimile of our own. No wonder I tried so hard to crawl under the refrigerator as a kid.

As you might imagine, roaches are survivors. You might complain about the number of candles on your birthday cake, but think what the cockroach has to go through. He's been around for over 350 million years. That's a heck of a lot of candles!

Actually, the heat from such a celebration would be an effective way to eliminate these voracious insects. Cockroaches will die when exposed to heat of 130 degrees Fahrenheit, but your house wiring, not to mention your family, pets, plants, electronic devices and furniture, may not be able to handle it either.

Roaches also die when the temperature drops to 23 degrees Fahrenheit for a long period of time. Leaving your windows open in freezing weather can eliminate roaches, but also a few of your fingers and toes as well.

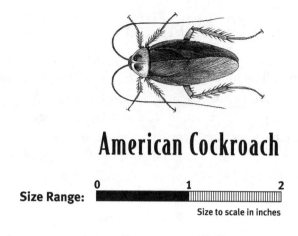

American Cockroach

Size Range:

0   1   2

Size to scale in inches

IDENTIFICATION & GENERAL INFORMATION

This roach is light brown in color and has a yellowish band on the back of its head. A very good flyer, it is frequently seen in the southern United States. The American cockroach usually stays outdoors, but during the warmer months of the year will enter even the cleanest of homes. They are attracted to dog food and usually invade the attic, garage, crawl spaces, and dense vegetation next to the home. This is the species of roach that helped me land an appearance on *The Tonight Show* with Johnny Carson.

PREVENTATIVE & LOW-IMPACT TREATMENT

Try to build them out. If your house has weep holes, cover them with copper mesh. You can buy copper mesh under the name Stuff-It, and one application lasts forever (copper mesh doesn't oxidize like steel wool).

Make sure to keep the area outside of the house clean, and don't store firewood next to the foundation.

Glue boards are also effective indoors.

CHEMICAL TREATMENT

Use a liquid-residual spray around the foundation. The use of baits such as Larva Lur in dense areas of outside vegetation, in attics, and crawl spaces is very helpful in keeping the population under control. When I find them in a home, they are normally under the kitchen sink. Empty all cabinets where pots and pans are stored and do a thorough crack and crevice treatment with a residual type of product. Be sure to treat the garage as well as all doorways that lead outside.

Inside treatment can also be done using bait stations, roach gels, and dusts such as boric acid or DE. Gel baits that contain hydramethylnon or Fipronil work pretty good, too. They can be found under the Combat label.

Tip: When using gel baits outside, I like to put them into the type of PVC tubing that is used for sprinkler systems. Cut the 1 inch wide tubing into 6 inch lengths. This keeps non-target animals away from the bait.

Cockroaches have been around nearly since the beginning of time. They have weathered floods, fires, famine— even ventures into outer space.

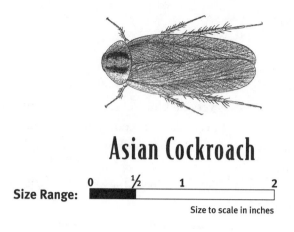

Asian Cockroach

Size Range:

| 0 | ½ | 1 | | 2 |

Size to scale in inches

IDENTIFICATION & GENERAL INFORMATION

This small brownish-colored roach is found only in Florida, and looks very much like the German roach. The main difference between the two is that the Asian variety likes to fly and is attracted to light. Many people in Florida even complain about this roach crawling across the screen while they're watching television.

Unlike most roaches, the Asian doesn't hide. It stays right out there in the open and dares you to stomp it. Apparently, it's not that easy because the population growth rate of the Asian roach is very high.

PREVENTATIVE & LOW-IMPACT TREATMENT

Try to build them out. Seal all cracks and crevices that may provide an entry point to your house, and repair holes in screening. Avoid turning on a lot of bright lights in the house at night as the Asian roach will come looking for the party. If they do get inside, glue boards are helpful in catching them.

CHEMICAL TREATMENT

Use a good residual-type insecticide spray on the foundation, doorways, outside window sills, and in any cracks and crevices. In addition, treat dirt and grass areas next to the house with a barrier treatment of granules. Once inside, a residual insecticide sprayed to the cracks and crevices of baseboards will solve the problem. Always follow all product label instructions.

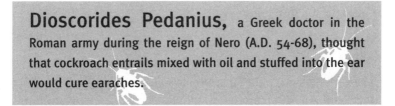

Dioscorides Pedanius, a Greek doctor in the Roman army during the reign of Nero (A.D. 54-68), thought that cockroach entrails mixed with oil and stuffed into the ear would cure earaches.

Australian Cockroach

| Size Range: | 0 | | 1 1¼ | | 2 |

Size to scale in inches

IDENTIFICATION & GENERAL INFORMATION

This large reddish-brown roach looks like the American variety, but is distinguished by a prominent pale yellow strip along the front of its wings. There is also a yellowish band on the back of its head.

PREVENTATIVE & LOW-IMPACT TREATMENT

This roach loves warm, humid weather with abundant plant material. As a result, if you live in the southern United States, or an equally humid region, you're asking for trouble if you situate plants right next to your house's foundation. Also, avoid wall-climbing vegetation.

Prevention is the key here. Trim all bushes and trees that are touching the house and check the seals on all doorways. The few roaches that get inside can be caught on glue boards.

CHEMICAL TREATMENT

Since this in an outside roach, you should concentrate your treatment on the foundation. Use a liquid-residual spray or, in areas of heavy infestation, a granular insecticide. Micro-encapsulated products will last much longer, so it makes sense to seek these out.

If your home has weep holes, you can dust them with DE or boric acid.

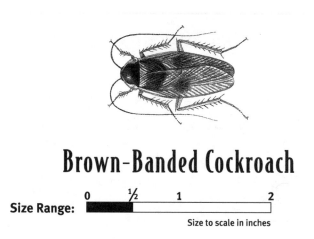

Brown-Banded Cockroach

Size Range:

| 0 | ½ | 1 | 2 |

Size to scale in inches

IDENTIFICATION & GENERAL INFORMATION

This small roach is mostly light brown in color, and is distinguished by two light-colored yellow strips on its wings. Normally not found on floors, this roach is a good climber and likes to hide behind wall-hanging pictures. The brown-banded variety is also notable in that it's found farther away from water sources than any other species of roach.

PREVENTATIVE & LOW-IMPACT TREATMENT

Start by carefully inspecting incoming provisions like groceries, firewood, playthings, or storage containers that have been outside for a while but now are being brought indoors. Tricky roaches like the brown-banded variety have an amazing knack for hitching a ride on just about anything to gain entry to a house.

Because this roach is a born climber, eliminating floor clutter like old grocery bags, cardboard boxes or other ground mess will not necessarily eliminate all brown-banded harborages. You must also check hanging pictures, plants and wall crevices for this pest. Sealing cracks and fissures along baseboards, pipe fittings and electrical outlets will also help eliminate potential roach hiding places.

CHEMICAL TREATMENT

The spot application of a liquid-residual spray in cracks and crevices will do in this roach. Because the brown-banded species is not a very common variety and has more of a random pattern of behavior, fogging may be needed to eradicate this pest. I normally don't like to recommenced fogging, but in some high population areas, a pyrethrum fogger that gives good contact kill but has no residual effects, could be used safely. Remember, follow all label directions closely.

Some baits that contain boric acid, hydramethylnon or Fipronil are also effective in controlling this roach.

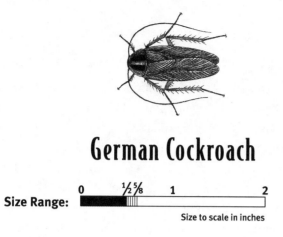

German Cockroach

Size Range:
```
0        ½ ⅝   1              2
■■■■■■■■■|||||□□□□□□□□□□□□□□□□□□
              Size to scale in inches
```

IDENTIFICATION & GENERAL INFORMATION

Achtung, this bug is a big 'un! Found worldwide, the German variety is the most common species of roach on the planet, and as such is a global headache of major proportions. Under ideal conditions, it only takes 30 days for this roach to go from an egg to an adult. It is the cause of many illnesses and allergic reactions in people, and will eat virtually anything. It especially likes books (the taste of binding paste is a delicacy!). Apparently, its favorites are *Tail of the Cockroach, Munching on the Grapes of Wrath,* and *Oedifice Wrecks.*

PREVENTATIVE & LOW-IMPACT TREATMENT

Sanitation is the key. Even the smallest crumbs of food will attract them. In addition, entry points in kitchens and bathrooms should be well-sealed. Don't forget to check the points where pipes enter plaster.

Because they like warm, humid environments, these roaches will also be found near stoves, sinks and dishwashers. Try to keep these areas from getting overly damp, and check regularly for signs of German roach infestations. If you can cover up or seal potential harborages in these environments, you may drive these roaches into the open, or back outside in search of moisture.

CHEMICAL TREATMENT

Forget the sprays here. The best plan of attack is to use a combination of bait stations or gels. The most effective contain hydramethylnon or fipronil.

The German cockroach can go without food for a month, but less than two weeks without water.

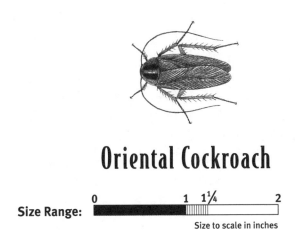

Oriental Cockroach

| | 0 | | 1 | 1¼ | | 2 |
Size Range: Size to scale in inches

IDENTIFICATION & GENERAL INFORMATION

This is a very dark, large and roundish roach that is almost solid black in color. It can be easily identified by the underdeveloped wings in both the male and female. The Oriental roach is found in basements, sewers, and other high-moisture areas.

Preventative & Low-Impact Treatment

Because this roach prefers damp environments, try to eliminate areas of moisture that would attract this species. Pay special attention to bathrooms, water-heaters, basements, attics and any other room where humidity may lead to dampness. The mulch in flower beds is a favorite outdoor habitat for this roach, so you should refrain from over-watering in this area.

By keeping flower plots and garden areas away from the foundation of your home, you'll also make it tougher for these suckers to enter your house in the first place.

Glue boards will trap any insects that get inside your home.

Chemical Treatment

Treatment to the outside of your house with a liquid-residual spray, as well as a granular insecticide sprayed over the foundation area, will keep most of these roaches from entering your home. Also, be sure to treat doorways and any cracks in the foundation.

I also recommend the use of gel baits that contain hydramethylnon or Fipronil. For added protection, you can dust plumbing voids with either boric acid or DE. Be careful when using these products, and always follow label instructions.

Pennsylvania Wood Roach

Size Range:

Size to scale in inches

IDENTIFICATION & GENERAL INFORMATION

This pencil-thin roach is tan colored, but at times appears dark brown. Because it is attracted to woodpiles, many infestations are the result of people bringing firewood into the home without first inspecting the logs for roaches. This species is also attracted to porch lights left on at night. While it does not breed inside the home, the Pennsylvania wood roach can still be an occasional invader.

PREVENTATIVE & LOW-IMPACT TREATMENT

Keeping woodpiles away from the house—including firewood, which should be stored outside of the house—will go a long way towards preventing this pest from getting inside your front door. Leaf litter and other good hiding places should also be picked up and disposed of regularly.

Be sure to check seals on all doorways and garage doors, and look for any foundation cracks or other possible points of entry. If any are found, quickly repair them with caulk or a well-secured patch. For the few roaches that do get inside, use glue boards to catch them.

CHEMICAL TREATMENT

During the warmer months of the year, you can use a liquid-residual spray to treat doorways, the foundation, and garage. If you find one of these roaches inside your house, consider a spot treatment to the infested areas. Always remember to use caution, and take all preventative steps necessary to ensure safe use of the product.

Cockroaches can run almost as fast as some speed limits—topping out at about 15 miles per hour.

Smoky Brown Cockroach

Size Range:

| 0 | | 1 | 1½ | 2 |

Size to scale in inches

IDENTIFICATION & GENERAL INFORMATION

This large, mahogany-brown roach lives outdoors, but will enter homes during the warmer months of the year. Normally it likes to live under leaf litter, around compost piles, and under wood decks. Many times these good flyers will glue their egg capsules to the sides of homes or garage walls. Since it takes a full year for this roach to reach adulthood from its larval stage, control of this species can be long-lasting if done correctly. This large roach is sometimes referred to as a "waterbug" by people who cannot accept the fact that they have roaches. Nevertheless, they are exactly the same thing.

PREVENTATIVE & LOW-IMPACT TREATMENT

Try to build this roach out of your house. You can prevent them from entering by using caulking (silicone) and copper mesh to seal all cracks or screen tears.

The use of glue boards will help catch those that make it inside. The proper placement areas of glue boards are the garage, under sinks, and behind washing machines. But be sure to place the boards in areas that won't attract pets.

CHEMICAL TREATMENT

Spraying the outside of the home with a long-lasting residual will eradicate many of the roaches before they move inside the home. Since most homes have a lot of ground cover next to the foundation, I like to place either bait or insecticide granules in these areas. Many times, this roach can be found in attic spaces as well as the crawl spaces underneath houses. In these areas, I recommend bait-type products or Catchmaster glue boards for long-lasting results.

In addition, the new gels that contain hydramethylnon or Fipronil are long-lasting and do a great job. The key to using the gels is to make a lot of bait placements, not just a few large ones.

Less toxic dusts such as boric acid or DE can also be very effective when applied to plumbing voids and external cracks and crevices.

COYOTES

As humans expand their cities and suburbs more and more into previously undeveloped terrain, wild predators like coyotes are doing what they have to do to survive in these new surroundings. Often, that means gulping up Whiskers or Spot as they scurry around the backyard of your suburban home.

Chemicals once used to kill coyotes have been banned by the federal government. Though the newer control devices are effective, the coyote is making a comeback in the United States. This is especially true here in Texas, where you can even spot coyotes running around pretty darn close to the Dallas-Fort Worth airport.

This slowly increasing coyote population presents problems that have to be addressed. Despite their inherent shyness and preference to hunt at night and early in the morning, coyotes are encroaching on human populations when they hunt rabbits and rodents in backyards, or sniff through trash cans for food. And, of course, they're not above making a dinner out of your cherished pet if you leave it alone outdoors.

So it's probably inevitable that we'll have more and more contact with these animals. Don't let their dog-like ways and bright eyes lull you into a false sense of domestic security; these are fierce hunters and will defend themselves if they feel threatened. If you live in coyote country, never let your toddlers or small children play outside unsupervised.

Coyote

Size: 3 to 4 feet long; 15 to 35 pounds.

IDENTIFICATION & GENERAL INFORMATION

Coyotes do look quite a bit like certain dog species with their fluffy tails, taut bodies, low howl and tawny color. A typical litter consists of six pups, with breeding season in late winter or early spring. Males and females usually raise their offspring together in secluded dens, in shelters already abandoned by another animal. In urban areas, coyotes tend to be found along washes, creeks or on the fringe of undeveloped areas.

PREVENTATIVE & LOW-IMPACT TREATMENT

If you have an enclosed backyard, make sure there are no gaps or holes in walls or fencing where a coyote can gain entry. Coyotes will sometimes dig their way under a perimeter, so keep an eye out for signs of tampering.

Keep your pets indoors at night if possible, and never let your children play outside alone. If you can trim the brush in your yard fairly thin, and remove potential yard cover for rabbits or mice, you can prevent coyotes from looking for these prey on your property. Also, cover and tightly seal all garbage containers so they don't tempt a coyote with their smell.

It should go without saying that you should never feed—or leave food out for—coyotes. You're just asking for trouble, and you'll usually get it. Also, don't feed your pet outside, and then leave the food out. Odds are, you'll have a new pet coyote before you know it.

Live-trapping this animal is difficult and probably not worth the effort. You'd just have to relocate the coyote anyway, and it would most likely end up in someone else's backyard. Call your local animal control department if you have coyote problems.

CHEMICAL TREATMENT

None

Buddy Holly and the Crickets had a good idea! Males of one North American cricket species attract females by singing in groups. Some of the males don't sing, though; they are groupies that hang out to meet girls.

CRICKETS

The pleasant chirping of the cricket is actually a mating call — the insect kingdom's equivalent of, "Hey, baby, what's your sign?" If you're not into hearing another life form getting more action than you are, and want to scare off the offending orthopteran insects, look for them under leaves and other organic matter.

Like a number of other insects, including moths and beetles, crickets like to feed on fabric. While they aren't found indoors very often, when they do march in, crickets will feast on cotton, wool, nylon, silk, leather and carpets. An expensive buffet, indeed.

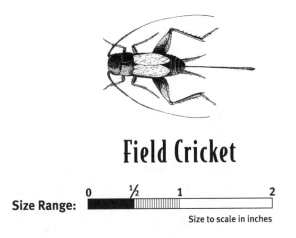

Field Cricket

Size Range:

| 0 | ½ | 1 | | 2 |

Size to scale in inches

IDENTIFICATION & GENERAL INFORMATION

This brownish or blackish-colored insect is a good flyer, which makes it difficult to eradicate. While the chirping of the male cricket may be tuneful at first, you might not like it if the music plays all night long. The sound is created when the cricket rubs its leg and wing together.

PREVENTATIVE & LOW-IMPACT TREATMENT

By trimming bushes in your yard, you will prevent these pests from congregating at home-entry points. Caulk all foundation cracks, and repair any tears in window screens. Keeping the crickets' focus outside your house with yellow-bulbed bug lights will also help.

For crickets that may wander inside, trap them with glue boards.

CHEMICAL TREATMENT

To prevent an indoor infestation, apply an approved residual insecticide to the outside of your home. Many times it will also be necessary to spread a three-foot swath of granules on the ground next to your foundation. Inside, apply spot treatments to the baseboards with a properly-labeled product.

You can also apply a spot treatment with synthetic pyrethroids to make sure they won't stay long.

The left hand doesn't know what the right hand is doing! Just like people, insects do have a preference that favors one side over the other. Crickets and grasshoppers are usually right-handed. They produce their chirp by rubbing the right wing over the left leg.

DEER

Like coyotes, deer are coming into increasing contact with humans as we move deeper and deeper into virgin forest lands. While deer won't hunt down your doggie or kitty like a coyote or wolf, they will damage trees, bushes and plants when they browse for food.

The most common deer across the United States is the white-tailed deer. Odds are you've seen this species looking for plants and veggies in the tree-heavy outskirts of your city, on the side of a highway, or lashed to the roof of an ATV with a pro-N.R.A. bumper sticker.

Deer

Size: 5 to 8 feet long; 50 to 300 pounds.

IDENTIFICATION & GENERAL INFORMATION

The most common species are usually brown to grey in color, with white tails. The males are distinguished from the females by their antlers and their boasts of being "more macho" when frozen in headlights. Deer are mostly active in the early morning and evening. They tend to live at the fringes of forests, using the denser areas as cover to escape from enemies and for shelter in winter. However, they come out into the open to forage. In addition to the grasses and plants they eat in the wild, deer are increasingly feasting on our farm crops like alfalfa, fruit, corn and grains.

PREVENTATIVE & LOW-IMPACT TREATMENT

Since these mammals are protected by state and federal laws, you should contact your local animal control department before trying to eliminate your deer problem.

In many cases, placing a low-voltage electric fence around your property may help prevent damage to your yard plants. If possible, protect fruit and vegetable garden crops with wire mesh or some other impenetrable perimeter.

Certain repellents are also effective. I've known a few people who've had good luck hanging small bottles of coyote urine around their yard. The idea here is that once a deer smells the scent of a predator, he-deer or she-deer will leave the area quickly before they become another animal's meal. Handfuls of human hair clippings in fine-mesh bags tied around your yard may also drive away deer. They either think we're the enemy, or else hate the smell o' Prell. Sometimes the hair thing works, sometimes it doesn't.

At this time, live capture and relocation of deer is very costly, with a very low survival rate.

CHEMICAL TREATMENT

There's a spray on the market called Deer-Away. It's said to repel most deer species with an 80-100% success rate. Make sure you don't buy the similarly labeled product, "Dear-Away," or your significant other may soon catch the first bus out of town.

EARWIGS

This insect gets unjustly blamed for causing a lot of trouble. Despite the common assumption, earwigs do not crawl into the ears of sleeping people. They leave that job up to the Wax Fairy. While earwigs can chew holes in fresh flowers and ripe fruit, their typical diet is rotting fruit, decaying litter, ants, snails and aphids. So, rather than doing a two-step in your auditory canals, these critters are actually out ridding the garden of some pretty annoying pests.

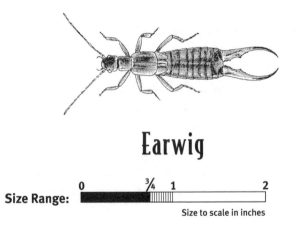

Earwig

Size Range: 0   ¾   1   2

Size to scale in inches

IDENTIFICATION & GENERAL INFORMATION

An earwig is dark brown in color and easy to identify by the pair of pincers at its rear. I always thought they were never used, until I picked one up and it pinched me, drawing blood. Take my word for it, leave those little suckers on the ground.

Earwigs typically live under the decayed bark of trees, beneath stones, or in old straw. Rarely does an earwig population grow so large that control measures are called for, although they do like to relax in the middle of flower blossoms, so some gardeners prefer to evict them. They also like to hide in places like a child's sandbox. To check if any are there, sift the sand through window screening to trap them, then crush any that appear.

In spring, earwig young hatch from eggs laid the previous fall. The young stay close to their underground nests for about two weeks, then make their first above-ground appearance in late April or early May. They typically enter the home by squeezing in under doorways.

PREVENTATIVE & LOW-IMPACT TREATMENT

You can trap earwigs pretty easily, without resorting to store-bought products or fancy chemical devices. Capitalizing on the insect's natural tendency to crawl into tight, hollow spaces, just take a cut-off section of garden hose, a length of bamboo, or even a sliced up Hula Hoop and place them in your yard next to plants you think have been damaged by earwigs. Give the pests a day or two to enter the traps, then pick them up and knock the bugs into the toilet or just crush them.

To prevent earwigs from entering your home, caulk all foundation cracks, and try to situate fruit trees and leafy plants a good distance from your house. If they do get in, get 'em with glue boards.

CHEMICAL TREATMENT

Use a residual chemical to spray the lower foundation of your house, making sure to treat the doorways as well. Dispersing a granular insecticide in the dirt area next to your house's foundation will help prevent reinfestation.

You can also dust any weep holes with DE or boric acid. Check the seals on all doorways and apply spot applications, if needed.

FLEAS

Instead of bombing fleas, you might want to open a circus with these insects as the star attraction. Certain kinds of fleas can actually be trained to jump through hoops, juggle, and pull objects several hundred times their own weight. Because fleas are so minuscule, human trainers usually need the help of a magnifying glass.

Despite winning fame as the blood-sucking parasite best known for biting cats, dogs, and humans, fleas can also attack birds. Quite an accomplishment. But since the majority of households in the United States include at least one cat or dog, it's easy to see why fleas are such a big annoyance to pets and people.

Flea infestations are at their worst during warm weather. Because these bugs lay most of their eggs when temperatures are above 85 degrees and the humidity is high, summer is the most acute season for scratching those flea bites. It's actually the toxins in flea saliva that cause severe itching and inflammation on the skin of people and pets. Some folks are even reluctant to own a pet because of a potential flea infestation. While it does take time and energy to control fleas, it can be done safely.

Fleas have been around for at least 60 million years. They can jump 150 times their own height. Even more impressive, they can jump thirty thousand times without stopping. If a man could jump proportionately as high, he would be able to leap almost to the top of the Empire State Building.

Flea

Size: 1/16 to 1/4 inch long.

IDENTIFICATION & GENERAL INFORMATION

Fleas are small and brownish colored. Despite being excellent jumpers, they mostly just bite humans on the ankles and feet.

Although development time varies due to temperature and humidity, fleas will eventually undergo a complete metamorphosis from larvae to ankle-biting adult. Under ideal conditions, full development can take as little as thirty days. A female flea may lay up to 200 eggs during her lifetime. But in order to do so, she must have a blood meal, from either people or pets.

PREVENTATIVE & LOW-IMPACT TREATMENT

Washing your pets with soapy water is sometimes enough to flush out fleas from their coats. If you've got the typical water-hating kitty, or a "bath-challenged" pup, fine-toothed flea combs are another great way to brush the squirming little buggers off your pet's skin.

Probably the best way to prevent fleas from getting a foothold in your yard is by not letting your pets run wild. Ninety percent of homes infested with these insects get them as a result of pets straying into areas where fleas thrive.

If you do find fleas in your house, vacuum infested rooms frequently, concentrating on upholstery crevices, carpet corners and floor cracks where the fleas, larvae and eggs may be camping out.

Chemical Treatment

To achieve optimum success, treat three areas simultaneously: the house, yard, and pet. In the house, foggers are not effective. In most cases, the chemical never gets to the areas where it will do the most good (i.e. under the furniture). Instead, select products that are labeled for complete floor treatment, not just spot treatment. Make sure to vacuum first, then throw away the bag. Then vacuum under all beds and furniture. Make sure to keep people and pets out of the infested area until the spray dries, and never apply any chemical to beds, food-storage areas or sensitive plants. Use a spray that contains an adullicide and an IGR (Insect Growth Regulator). This will prevent reinfestation for up to six months. A single application, however, is usually all that's needed. Vacuuming every day for one week after treatment will cause the pupa stage to hatch, leading to a much quicker resolution of your flea problem.

In the yard, a liquid-type residual product applied in a hose-end sprayer will give you the best results. Don't use a pump sprayer to treat a yard; it won't work. Make sure the grass is cut and all toys and other items are picked up. The best time for treatment is early or late in the day, when the sun is not at its peak. During the warmer periods of the year, monthly application is recommended. Be sure to keep off of the grass until it is dry.

Your pet should be professionally treated. If you want to treat your pets yourself, just go to any pet supply store and ask for the most effective spray, dip or dust. Note: Never use a dog dip for a cat; in some cases, it could be deadly.

Adult fleas can live up to one and on-half years before feeding. They must feed, however, before mating.

FLIES

It's likely that over a million species of flies exist in the world today, not counting Jeff Goldblum in that cheesy movie with Geena Davis. Most flies have spherical heads, big eyes and antennae. In males, hair covers the antennae, except for the infamous Fly Sperling ("I'm not only the president, I'm also a member."). Word's out on the long-term profit potential for the Hair Club for Flies.

It is the fly's suction-equipped mouth that enables it to take in food. In some species of fly, the mouth is even able to pierce skin in order to reach the blood beneath it. So the next time your buddy tells you, "Flies suck, man!," you can tell him he's absolutely right.

While these winged insects may play an important role in the balance of nature, they can also carry diseases. And when they get into our homes the risk of contamination is great, particularly on food products.

This is a result of the fact that many species of fly lay their eggs in cesspools, stagnant water, garbage cans or rotting matter. Hanging out in these lovely places, it's no wonder bacteria enter their bodies and become trapped on their leg hairs. Fly larvae (maggots) vary in size and shape, but are always laid in great numbers.

I'm sure I don't have to tell you that flies have an excellent sense of smell and are attracted to most food aromas, especially unpleasant ones. Spoiled food is a fly's feast. Therefore, proper sanitation in indoor and outdoor areas is the key to controlling flies. The proper disposal of pet droppings is also important.

Many times, it will take more than just your efforts to eradicate a fly problem on your property. You may have to work closely with a neighbor or neighbors to clean up the immediate area surrounding your home.

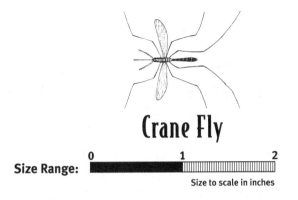

Crane Fly

Size Range:

0   1   2

Size to scale in inches

IDENTIFICATION & GENERAL INFORMATION

This huge fly actually looks like a giant mosquito. Don't worry too much, though. The crane fly doesn't have any biting mouth parts. The wings have a distinct ribbed pattern and the legs are extremely long. This is normally the first fly to emerge in the spring and will usually cluster at the entrances to your home. Moist areas behind bushes will also attract this pest.

PREVENTATIVE & LOW-IMPACT TREATMENT

Avoid over-watering your lawn or potted yard plants. This fly is attracted to dampness like some other species are attracted to garbage and feces. If you can maintain a buffer between your home and yard—a concrete walk, gravel path, etc.—all the better. Probably the best way to keep these flies from becoming pestiferous is to keep them outside your house. Self-closing screen doors are a great help in the hotter months. They will let air in, but keep bothersome flies out. Never allow these flies unimpeded access to your home. If you find holes in window screens or screen doors, repair them immediately. For the few crane flies that do sneak in, go after them with your trusty fly swatter.

CHEMICAL TREATMENT

None

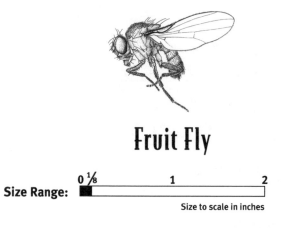

Fruit Fly

Size Range:

0 ⅛   1   2

Size to scale in inches

IDENTIFICATION & GENERAL INFORMATION

This very small fly is a pest in kitchens and other areas where you keep overripe fruit such as bananas. The fruit fly is tan or brown in color, with bright red eyes. Once you determine that your produce-muncher is a fruit fly, search for the ripe fruit source. In addition to bananas, this fly favors pineapples, potatoes and beer cans left in recycling bins. The adult flies are also attracted to light. And I don't mean light beer.

PREVENTATIVE & LOW-IMPACT TREATMENT

Before any type of control is started, find the infestation source and get rid of it. This will not only help eradicate your current problem, but will also prevent fruit flies from entering your home again. If possible, cut these flies off at the pass by eliminating outdoor attractants. Tightly seal all garbage cans and bags, pick up any tree-fallen fruit, and keep your yard free of garden clippings and plant debris.

CHEMICAL TREATMENT

After you locate the source, use an approved flying insect spray, following label directions closely. Pyrethrum is good because it will quickly knock down the adult population, but won't leave a residue.

The use of light traps also works well in commercial settings. A small plastic trapping jar with a special one-way lid can be found at most hardware stores or specialty pest control supply stores. Bait these traps with pieces of banana.

Fly ball! If all the offspring of a pair of fruit flies survived and mated, the 25th generation—just one year later—would form a ball of flies that would almost reach from the earth to the sun.

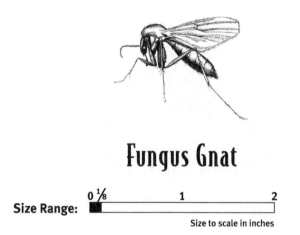

Fungus Gnat

Size Range: 0 ⅛   1   2

Size to scale in inches

IDENTIFICATION & GENERAL INFORMATION

This tiny black fly resembles a mosquito, but is much smaller. This gnat likes to infest moist, shaded areas. A natural fungi will be present wherever there is high organic material, and this is what attracts the fungus gnat. Potted plants are probably the main source of home infestation.

PREVENTATIVE & LOW-IMPACT TREATMENT

Prevention on the outside of the home is the key. Correct poor drainage areas and avoid over-watering landscape plants. If you notice a build up of fungi in a particular area of your yard or garden, watch that parcel closely for gnat infestation. If you notice the presence of these tiny critters, either remove the infested plant, or try to eliminate some of the moistness in the area.

CHEMICAL TREATMENT

For fungus gnats that get inside plants, use Schultz Plant Spray (active ingredient: pyrethrum). You will need to treat the source of infestation for several days. Plan on spraying the dirt in the plant for 2 to 3 days in a row.

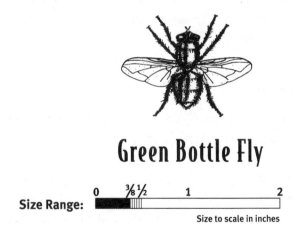

Green Bottle Fly

Size Range:

0   3/8 1/2   1   2

Size to scale in inches

IDENTIFICATION & GENERAL INFORMATION

This medium-sized fly is metallic green or blackish in color. Hordes of them seemingly show up at once for no apparent reason. Most will be found near the windows of your home and are easy to eradicate with a fly swatter. Many times the larvae, or maggots, can be found crawling on countertops or carpets. Most infestations are the result of a dead animal—such as a rat—rotting away silently in the attic. This is why many homeowners report seeing maggots falling out of recessed ceiling lights or air conditioning vents.

PREVENTATIVE & LOW-IMPACT TREATMENT

Get out the fly swatter and have some fun!

Actually, the key is to locate the dead animal. The rancid smell will usually lead you to it. Disregard this when the man of the house is watching Monday Night Football on the couch.

When you find your decomposing friend, use rubber gloves, a good flashlight and plastic bags to scoop up the debris. Be prepared: When you find the animal, it will be surrounded by swarming flies and maggots. A small amount of Nil-Odor, available in hardware stores, will help neutralize the smell. Look for the Nil-Odor that comes in a wick container.

CHEMICAL TREATMENT

If you feel it's necessary to disperse the swarm, use a fogger in the infested area. Read the label and follow all printed instructions carefully.

Alternatively, make a spot application with a pyrethrum aerosol. Following label instructions, you'll most likely need to apply product near the windows in an infested room and then leave the area for about an hour.

House Fly

Size Range: 0 ⅛¼   1   2

Size to scale in inches

IDENTIFICATION & GENERAL INFORMATION

This small fly is gray to black in color, with two stripes on its face.
A house fly infestation will usually mean a preponderance of larvae, also called maggots. They are cream colored and can be
found crawling on the floor or near the garbage bin.

Flies generally enter your home through an open door or
window, after being attracted by the smell of ripe garbage. It takes
just one week for the eggs of this pest to hatch into maggots. Since
flies have sponging mouths, they tend to feed on liquid or moist
items. Many people who keep a dog in the yard but don't clean
up after Fido will also have a problem with house flies.

PREVENTATIVE & LOW-IMPACT TREATMENT

The key in any kind of fly control is the elimination of the larval
breeding sites. Proper sanitation will remove much of the problem. You can also build them out. Check for holes in screens and
keep doors closed as much as possible. Once they get inside the
home, use a fly swatter.

A number of sticky fly tubes are available; a good one I have
used is called Musca Stick. If you use a fly trap, you'll notice that

the manufacturer has included a packet of sex pheromones. Do not use these on your special someone! Instead, sprinkle the packet's contents on the glue and the flies will dive-bomb the stick.

If you have an ongoing problem, purchase a good insect zapper at a supply store such as Home Depot or Lowe's. As a decent last-resort treatment, try keeping planters of basil and sage around the house. Flies hate these herbs.

CHEMICAL TREATMENT

As a last-resort option, spraying should be limited to spot applications with a pyrethrum-based product. As always, follow all label instructions carefully.

🎬🎬🎬🎬 Movie Review 🎬🎬🎬🎬

The Fly (1986)—I have to admit, I didn't see the original version of this movie, only the remake with Jeff Goldblum and Geena Davis. Basically, in this film Goldblum's a scientist who builds this transporter machine but accidentally gets caught in it with a fly. Pretty soon, he starts sprouting hair in weird places and finally becomes a full-fledged Fly Guy. The special effects and make-up were really good, but the whole mushy love angle sorta chapped my hide. Where I live, the only emotional and physical contact we have with houseflies is when our swatters smoosh them against a wall.

(All reviews are on a scale of 1 to 5 roaches, with 5 being best.)

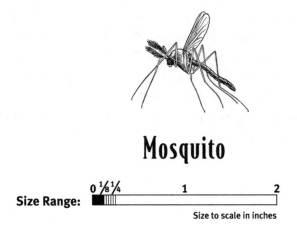

Mosquito

Size Range: 0 ⅛¼   1   2

Size to scale in inches

IDENTIFICATION & GENERAL INFORMATION

Mosquitoes are small flies (their name is actually Spanish for "little fly") that have a piercing mouthpart which allows them to break skin and suck out small amounts of blood. Although both sexes feed on the nectar of flowers, the male never bites a host. However, without a fresh blood meal, the female mosquito cannot lay eggs.

Without a doubt, this delicate little insect is one of the most dangerous pests on earth. There are anywhere from 3,000 to 4,000 different mosquito species—125 in the United States alone—and almost 500 of them are capable of transmitting diseases.

In warmer climates, mosquitoes will be present all year. In colder regions, the bugs usually start suckin' as early as February, when melting snow creates pools that are perfect places for the female to shelter her eggs.

PREVENTATIVE & LOW-IMPACT TREATMENT

Cities once used helicopters or specially-equipped trucks to dispense large amounts of chemicals in the air to eradicate the adult mosquito population. For the most part, that practice has been stopped. The best way to control these flies nowadays is to eliminate their breeding sites. That means getting rid of standing water, if possible. The introduction of a mosquito-eating fish called Gambusia in small ponds works wonders. Also, try planting some basil, rosemary, garlic or onion in your garden. These have all been proven to gross out the occasional skeeter and drive them elsewhere.

As long as you're at it, you should try to repair all screen doors and window screens on your house. And if you're going camping, don't forget to bring a tent with mosquito netting.

CHEMICAL TREATMENT

Mosquito dunks are quite useful. They are larvacides that are poured into mosquito breeding grounds and halt reproduction (usually with an insect growth regulator). Pick them up at your local pest control store or home-supply center.

Also, a portable butane fogger sold by the Burgess company gives off a heavy, white non-residual insecticide that will kill mosquitoes on contact.

When outdoors, there are several effective mosquito repellents. Off is a product that works quite well.

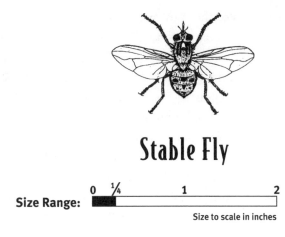

Stable Fly

Size Range: 0 ¼   1   2

Size to scale in inches

IDENTIFICATION & GENERAL INFORMATION

This is a grayish-colored insect that looks like a house fly. Should it land on you, however, you'll know the difference immediately when it jabs its long proboscis into your skin. Their bites are very painful—similar to when the doctor pokes you with a needle. This fly can be found along beaches, as well as in stables and other animal holding bins. Usually an outside fly, they'll sometimes enter homes through open doors.

PREVENTATIVE & LOW-IMPACT TREATMENT

This fly is difficult to control because it's mainly found outside. Prevention is the key. Check all window screens for tears and repair them. If you have animals that spend a good deal of time outside, be sure to pick up and dispose of their droppings quickly. The longer that smell wafts around Flyville, the greater the likelihood that Mr. and Mrs. Stable Fly will get a whiff and buzz over for a closer look.

An electric "bug zapper" can be used to eradicate those that get inside. Also, a number of fly tubes are available. These two-foot long cylinders are covered with a sticky glue that attracts the flies, and traps them when they land.

Chemical Treatment

If you choose a fly spray, use one that contains pyrethrum. Read and follow all label instructions.

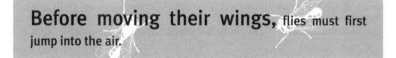

Before moving their wings, flies must first jump into the air.

GOPHERS

If you've got a vegetable garden, odds are you've seen the damage a hungry gopher can cause firsthand. These plump mammals eat a variety of plants, including bulbs, tubers, roots and some grasses. While they occasionally come above ground to feed on herbaceous plants, most gopher meals are underground. Because they don't hibernate, these animals must hoard food to survive over the winter.

Unless you're a gopher, you'd probably think their lives are pretty dismal. They stay underground almost exclusively in burrows dug 6 to 18 inches below the soil surface. Gophers only come together for mating in the spring and early summer. Information is sketchy whether they shower and floss before this rendezvous.

Even though you may have many gopher mounds in your yard, it's likely that only one gopher is terrorizing your garden. Because they are territorial animals, they operate on a Eastwoodian "this yard isn't big enough for the both of us" mentality.

The mounds are created when the gopher throws out dirt as he enlarges his burrow. Be careful not to confuse gopher mounds with molehills. While the former look like little mountain caves with a closed burrow (plug) on the end, molehills have the appearance of small volcanoes, with their exit hole in the center of the mound, rather than the side. (Please see "Moles" entry later in the encyclopedia.)

Gopher

Size: 5 to 16 inches long; 6 to 8 ounces.

IDENTIFICATION & GENERAL INFORMATION

Gophers are thickset, with small eyes and ears, short necks and long, continuously growing front teeth for chomping down on roots and tubers. They are also characterized by long front claws, and fur-lined cheek pouches for food storage.

Unless a gopher is wreaking havoc on your garden, there's no need to eradicate it. Their burrows actually add helpful organic matter to the soil, and also help aerate it.

PREVENTATIVE & LOW-IMPACT TREATMENT

Various species of gopher have particular plants they find distasteful and offensive. For example, the western pocket gopher hates oleander. Also, most gophers will thumb their little button noses at castor beans. Ask a local garden expert which plant native to your area is mucho yucky for your gopher buddy.

In order to use short-term controls like flooding, fumigation and trapping, you first have to locate the main burrow. It's usually located a foot from the mound plug. Poke a stick around the mound until it sinks a couple inches; that's the main burrow.

To flood it, expose an entry tunnel to the mound and stick the hose end there, covering it up with dirt. When you turn on the water, the gopher will likely scurry to the surface.

Fumigation requires you to use a commercial gas cartridge or smoke bomb set off in the plug. Cover the hole to prevent smoke from escaping. Do not use gas when holes are next to a foundation.

Traps are useful for small-scale infestations. They're most effective when placed in the main burrow, which you should expose only long enough to insert two traps. Then, cover up the hole with dirt or a board. If you want to go medieval on the gopher, attach the traps to a stake in the ground so the critter can't drag them away.

CHEMICAL TREATMENT

Poison baits are available. However, since they are dangerous to non-target animals, I don't recommend using them.

LICE

Although most assume this wingless insect only attacks people with poor hygiene, lice are not picky. They like everyone! And because humans are warm-blooded, lice are able to breed year-round.

Specific species of lice are easy to identify. Head lice leave brown fecal material on the shoulders and back, which shows up easily on light-colored clothing. This is the most common variety of lice in the United States—the kind often transmitted amongst school children.

Body lice deposit dirty brown droppings around the armpits. Meanwhile, dark spots on your undergarments are a sign of pubic lice—also known as crabs. In addition, itching will be quite severe.

Crabs spend their entire lives on their host, while body lice hide in clothing when not feeding. Some people try to rid themselves of lice by taking a hot shower, which will not work. Lice have claws that are perfect for clinging to human hair, not to mention the fact that they don't easily drown and can survive hot temperatures. The eggs of lice are called "nits" and are glued to the shafts of hair.

Bright light causes lice to move quickly. However they don't jump or fly. But if you can somehow manage to dislodge the lice from your body, the bugs will die.

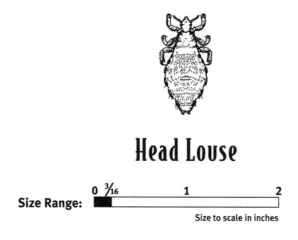

Head Louse

Size Range:

0 3/16   1   2

Size to scale in inches

Identification & General Information

Varying in color from off-white to a darkish gray, these extremely small insects just love to cling to hair follicles. For some reason, this species of louse only infests the hairs found on the head. Lice eggs become glued to the shafts of hair and are clearly visible under magnification.

Most lice infestations are found at schools or child-care centers, where the bugs are transmitted from child to child like answers to that night's homework assignment. Itching caused by lice is the result of the adult louse sucking the host's blood up through their scalp. Yum, yum!

Preventative & Low-Impact Treatment

Several shampoos and lotions are designed to eradicate head lice. Consult your doctor or pharmacist for a recommendation, then read and follow all label instructions.

In addition, wash all bedding in hot water, as well as anything that has touched the hair of the infested person. Don't forget to sanitize all hair grooming items, including combs and brushes.

Chemical Treatment

Fogging your house is a waste of money and is unnecessary. Head lice will die once they're off a human host anyway. Control should be done to the head. The most well-known product is called Rid or Nix.

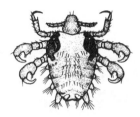

Crab (Pubic) Louse

Size: 1/16 inch long.

Identification & General Information

These are definitely not the pricey crustaceans you save for a candlelit dinner with your significant other. These are actually those itchy little buggers you gave to your significant other.

This louse got its name, as you might imagine, because it looks almost exactly like a miniature crab—except without the butter and lemon. They are usually grayish in color and very hard to see with the "naked" eye (pun intended). Crabs are found only in the pubic area and can cause excessive itching. The eggs, called nits, become glued to hair follicles, and are quite difficult to dislodge.

Preventative & Low-Impact Treatment

Check with your doctor or pharmacist for the best product. As of this writing, lotions and shampoos are the best treatment. Follow all label instructions, and don't forget to wash underwear and bed linens in hot water several times. Also, you may want to avoid that sleazy waterfront bar next time around.

CHEMICAL TREATMENT

Check with your doctor first. One must be careful when using chemicals "down there." Treatment is centered around the host, not the house.

A **dictionary-style** listing of all known insects would be six thousand pages long.

MITES

While there are a large number of beneficial species of mites, a few have the potential to cause lots of damage to your home and garden. The most prevalent pestiferous mites are the spider mites, broad mites, and cyclamen mites.

Spider mites, the most common mite pest, live in colonies and create small webs beneath a leaf or new plant growth before feeding. Broad and cyclamen mites are a quarter of the size of spider mites, making them almost invisible to the naked eye.

Mites seem to cause problems wherever they go—in the garden, in the kitchen, and in the ears of cats and dogs. It is estimated that half of all cats have mites at some time in their lives. Mites dig into the cat's ear and feed on the lymph of pierced cells. Severe attacks can permanently damage the middle ear, which may result in the cat holding its head to one side while walking in circles. Ear canker can also occur from heavy scratching and, if left untreated, can result in a cat's hearing loss.

In the garden, mites feed on flowers, the blossom ends of fruit, and bulbs. It is best to start watching for mites in the spring, when buds start to open. Mites can destroy many varieties of plants, including cotton. Signs of infestation include silver or yellow streaks or red spots on the upper half of leaves. Eventually, the affected leaves will curl and probably fall off the branch.

In the kitchen, mites will eat virtually anything, including cheese and wine. They also like to climb the walls, maybe as a result of all that cabernet. Susceptible foods include dried fruits, flour, meat, cheese, grains, caramel, fermenting substances, nuts and mushrooms, among others. Signs of mite infestation in foods are a pink or grayish dust scattered around the food. There may also be a strong or minty odor.

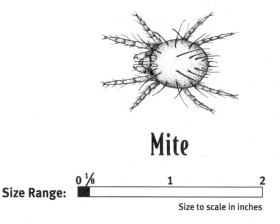

Mite

Size Range: 0 ⅛   1   2

Size to scale in inches

IDENTIFICATION & GENERAL INFORMATION

Mites are translucent, with sparse body hair. These pests can be trouble for humans, causing dermatitis and kidney problems.

Mites are most often found in bird nests, but spread easily and can be brought into the home on clothing. These tiny critters are often confused with ticks; both have the head, thorax, and abdomen connected on one unsegmented body. Mites, however, are typically much smaller than ticks.

PREVENTATIVE & LOW-IMPACT TREATMENT

Use mineral oil to treat infestations in your pet's ears. Apply the oil with an eyedropper and massage the outside of the ear to work the oil into the ear canal. Repeat this process every few days for best results.

For garden mites, hose down the infected plants with water as soon as you notice an infestation. This will knock off the mites and sometimes kill them. Be sure to spray the undersides of the leaves as well. Note: Garden mites have many natural predators—including lacewings, thrips, midges and ladybug beetles—so make sure to give these enemies time to get your mites before you go to the trouble of doing it.

In the kitchen, rotate your food products and discard all molding items. Also try to keep your cupboards clean and dry.

CHEMICAL TREATMENT

For pet ear infestations, Otomite-Plus works quite well. Consult a veterinarian for more information or to get a prescription.

In the garden, use a chemical spray only if your mite infestation is severe. Dust or spray the undersides of infested leaves with sulfur. Wear a dust mask if you use a powder, rubber gloves if you use a liquid. You can also use a pyrethrum-based product, but be aware that this may kill natural enemies as well as pest mites.

The second leading allergy in the United States—house dust—is caused by an eight-legged animal (the house dust mite) that is no bigger than the period at the end of this sentence.

MOLES

These small, squat mammals are perfectly designed for burrowing under the ground and eating stuff. Although their meals of choice are primarily insects like white grubs, earthworms and spiders, moles can cause the homeowner problems by invading and digging through lawns in search of food.

These animals are pretty versatile, constructing deep, permanent burrows up to three feet under the soil for living and raising young (let's call them "condos"), and shallow, feeding burrows just below the ground surface (let's call them "diners"). While they use the condos all the time, some diners are only used once and then abandoned.

When they exit the ground, they leave holes called molehills, which look like miniature volcanoes. But they can also disturb your lawn and garden when they burrow, creating raised ridges all throughout your yard.

Because moles are so active, working round-the-clock to expand their burrow systems and look for food, some species must consume more than their body weight in food each day to thrive. Hey, "the mole the merrier!"

Mole

Size: 6 to 8 inches long; 4 to 8 ounces.

IDENTIFICATION & GENERAL INFORMATION

These critters are born diggers, with pointy heads, no external ears, and short front legs. They have broad claws for shoveling, and fur that easily brushes in any direction.

They are found mostly in soft, crumbly soil, through which they can often swim. Because different species of moles can survive in so many different soil conditions, they pose a problem for people in almost every climate and terrain.

PREVENTATIVE AND LOW-IMPACT TREATMENT:

Although mole burrow ridges can be an eyesore, try to tolerate them as much as possible. Moles feed voraciously on many soil pests, and can really be a godsend for the home gardener.

To discourage moles from entering your yard in the first place, use soils that are highly compacted, heavy in clay or filled with rocks and stones that the critters can't dig through.

If moles already have invaded your lawn or garden and you really, really want to get rid of the suckers, you can use flooding, trapping or fumigating to get them out. (See section on flooding and fumigating in "Gophers" chapter for techniques.)

There are many different types of mole traps on the market. The best one I have seen is a spear-type trap from the Victor company. The traps are placed in the mole's runways. Then, when he comes back through the tunnel, he hits the trigger and it's "sayonara, Mole-San." Live traps won't work with this creature.

CHEMICAL TREATMENT

New to the market is a product by Dr T's called Whole. It is made of 100% castor oil and is watered into the lawn. When the mole eats worms or grubs that have this oil on them, it will give him a hardy dose of diarrhea. He probably won't return for more.

MOTHS

These insects have the distinction of being both pantry and clothes pests, depending on the species. You have to give the moth credit for having good taste. It dines on only the finest fur, wool, feathers and down items.

In the kitchen, moth larvae spin cocoons in food products, which destroys them quickly. Just about anything edible is susceptible, although pantry moths usually prefer dried foodstuffs. If you find little "white worms" in your food items, you've got moth problems.

The meal moths' clothes-loving cousins are most often attracted to wearables that have been stored for an extended period. These are most likely the things you don't have the heart to throw away, until you see a bunch of nasty moth holes in them.

Carpeting where there is no foot traffic is another spot moths will look to feed.

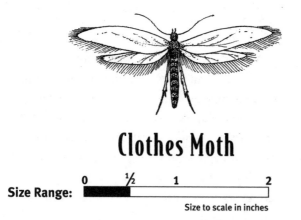

Clothes Moth

Size Range:

| 0 | ½ | 1 | | 2 |

Size to scale in inches

IDENTIFICATION & GENERAL INFORMATION

The adult clothing moth is a goldish color, while its larvae is usually white. The moth's larval stage does all the damage to your clothes. Sometimes, you know you have a problem when you spot a moth or two, but most often you get the drift when you go to put on your nice blouse and it looks like a piece of Swiss cheese.

Most infestations of this moth will occur in closets. During the summer when doors are left open, large grayish moths will frequently enter the home. While these are a nuisance, they cause no harm to clothes.

The clothes moth, however, cannot survive solely on clean items. Its nutrition also comes from food and drink stains, and even perspiration.

PREVENTATIVE & LOW-IMPACT TREATMENT

If you have a moth-infested closet, be sure to inspect the clothes and remove all items that are made of some type of hair. It is the keratin in hair that attracts the insects. It is very important to find the infested clothing and have it dry-cleaned. In some cases, the clothes will have to be thrown away. The next step is to vacuum any visible adults. Cedar closets help repel fabric-destroying pests. Keep this in mind if you ever build a home, or are adding on to your bedroom.

CHEMICAL TREATMENT

Never set off a fogger in a closet, as it will almost certainly damage your clothes. You might want to first try special clothing moth traps that are essentially made with glue that contains a sex pheromone as the attractant. If you must use a chemical, an aerosol pyrethrum spray used properly will eradicate adult moths. Alternatively, use a liquid-residual spray to treat the cracks and crevices of baseboards and shelving. As always, follow all label instructions carefully.

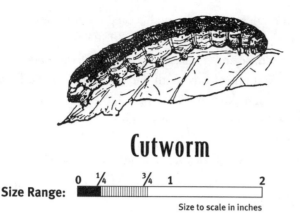

Cutworm

Size Range: 0 ¼ ¾ 1 2

Size to scale in inches

IDENTIFICATION & GENERAL INFORMATION

These small caterpillars—the larvae of certain moth species—destroy young plants by nibbling at the seedling's base. Cutworm damage will result in horizontal, lawnmower-type damage to ground-level plants. Go into your garden at night and look for the caterpillars curled up in the shape of a "C." If you see a bunch of 'em, you've got cutworm problems.

PREVENTATIVE & LOW-IMPACT TREATMENT

These little wigglers have lots of natural enemies. Use a mulch, or some other ground cover, to attract the ground beetles, toads or snakes which prey on cutworms. In autumn, make sure to clear away all weeds and plant debris where the adult cutworm moth lays its eggs.

When you see lots of little "C"s on your low-lying plants, you can either pluck them off at night, or spray them with BT.

CHEMICAL TREATMENT

The use of BT is very effective on cutworms. You might also try a product called Specricide or Dursban to eradicate this pest. Follow all instructions carefully.

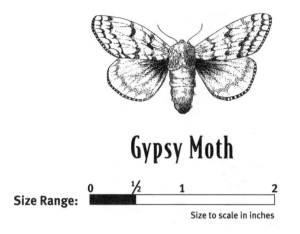

Gypsy Moth

Size Range:

| 0 | ½ | 1 | | 2 |

Size to scale in inches

IDENTIFICATION & GENERAL INFORMATION

Contrary to popular belief, this hungry little pest did not get its name by pestering European tourists for loose change. Rather, the gypsy moth is a major forest pest and is capable of defoliating millions of trees. While the trees rarely die, they nonetheless become eyesores and are more susceptible to disease.

PREVENTATIVE & LOW-IMPACT TREATMENT

Look for this moth's egg masses on outdoor items like building or camping equipment, toys or garden furniture. Usually, you can just rub off the masses with a damp cloth or blast them with a hose spray.

You can also protect your trees by banding them with a sticky tape or paper on the tree base.

CHEMICAL TREATMENT

As the U.S. Forest Service learned, pesticides just aren't that effective on this pest. Years of carbaryl spraying, then later, application of *bacillus thuringiensis* and *Dimilan,* killed a lot of moths, but killed the beneficial insects that hunt them as well. The result was a compounding of the problem.

For the average homeowner without a forest in their backyard, the low-impact measures should prove sufficient to controlling gypsy moths.

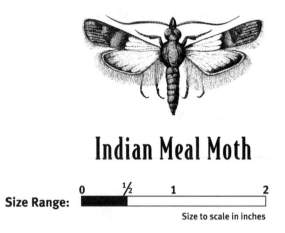

Indian Meal Moth

Size Range:

0　　½　　1　　　　　2

Size to scale in inches

IDENTIFICATION & GENERAL INFORMATION

This copper or grayish-colored moth has a light-colored band on the wings, and usually infests flour, corn meal, nuts, chocolate, dog food and, occasionally, whole grains. The larvae can be found in silken cocoons where the wall meets the ceiling, or in the corners of shelves. These pests stay mostly in the pantry, but will fly around the kitchen when the infestation level is high. Check all pantry products for the webbing that is a telltale sign of an Indian meal moth invasion.

PREVENTATIVE & LOW-IMPACT TREATMENT

Remove all of the food in the pantry and wash every shelf with warm, soapy water. As you replace the food packages on the shelves, carefully check them for infestation. Throw away all infested products in a tightly-sealed garbage bag, and dispose of it immediately.

A pantry pest trap with a pheromone disk is available in stores. Flying adult moths will be attracted by the pheromone, and get stuck on the glue. This renders them unable to lay more eggs. These traps will offer control for three to six months.

To prevent a flour infestation, many people store their flour in the freezer.

CHEMICAL TREATMENT

None. Never spray chemicals in food storage areas.

OPOSSUMS

Contrary to popular belief, these mammals were not created after Adam lovingly addressed Eve as "Oh, Possum!" Actually, this animal is the only marsupial in North America. The female—like her cousin the kangaroo—has an abdominal pouch for transporting her offspring.

While opossums can often be helpful around the garden by eating insects and crustaceans, they also damage lawns in search of grubs, or by entering crawl spaces, garages and other residential harborages. Their repulsive, musk-like odor alerts homeowners to their presence after party guests repeatedly ask to borrow the plunger and no one has even gone to the bathroom.

These nocturnal, secretive animals can be quite sluggish, choosing to lodge in hollow logs, under buildings, in garages, and even in abandoned squirrels' nests and woodchuck burrows.

Opossum

Size: 24 to 30 inches long, including tail; 10 to 20 pounds.

IDENTIFICATION & GENERAL INFORMATION

This grayish-colored marsupial looks like a giant rat. Generally most active at night, opossums prefer to sleep during the day. Since an opossum's sense of smell is acute, it can easily find food and will eat virtually anything it finds. Being excellent climbers, these animals enter most homes through roof holes, some measuring just four to six inches wide.

Most calls I get about this pest are from people complaining about opossums eating their dog's food. Hey, it could be worse. They could be eating the dog, too.

PREVENTATIVE & LOW-IMPACT TREATMENT

Eliminating outdoor harborages like hollow logs and unsealed crawl spaces is a good preventative measure to keep these marsupials from hanging around.

Once opossums enter your attic or garage, trapping is the best way to handle them. I like to use a large cage trap that measures 26 x 9 x 9 inches. Bait can be anything from sardines in oil to loganberries. Put the trap in an area where you've heard the animal scurrying about at night. Look for the Tomahawk trap. It has a sliding rear door to ease the release of the animal.

If you catch an opossum, take care not to touch its feces, which can contain a large amount of ectoparasites. For all you obsessive opossum feces-touchers, get some professional help.

After the animal is removed, sanitize the trap with bleach and water and reset it. If you can manage to find the hole your trapped opossum entered through, stuff it full with newspaper. If the paper is moved the next day, it means more of the critters are on the loose. Contact your local animal control officer to find out where to release opossums, or have them come and pick it up.

If you don't want to trap them, wait until night when they have left their nesting site and plug the hole. Since the hands of an opossum are probably not strong enough to open your patch, they will likely move somewhere else.

CHEMICAL TREATMENT

None

PILLBUGS AND SOWBUGS

Some people call these critters wood lice, ballbugs, rolly-pollies, or any number of descriptive names. Actually, these creatures aren't bugs at all, but are actually more closely related to crustaceans like lobsters and crabs.

The only discernible difference between pillbugs and sowbugs is that the former curls itself into a little ball when threatened. When sowbugs are threatened, they call 911.

If populations are high they will damage your young plants. For the most part, they're useful scavengers who convert decaying organic matter into soil nutrients. However, if your yard becomes too damp and attracts an overabundance of these little suckers, there's a risk they'll come into your house.

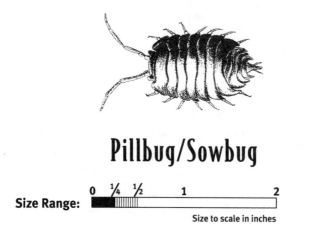

Pillbug/Sowbug

Size Range: 0   ¼   ½   1   2

Size to scale in inches

IDENTIFICATION & GENERAL INFORMATION

Both are grayish-colored pests and considered to be land crustaceans. They are slow-moving, and generally benign, unless their numbers grow too large.

PREVENTATIVE & LOW-IMPACT TREATMENT

Since this pest needs a lot of moisture to survive, keep debris such as rocks and leaf litter picked up, and don't over-water your garden. Also, plant flowers and shrubs far enough from your house so that the foundation remains dry.

Should these creatures venture inside, just vacuum them up. Small glue boards will also do the trick.

CHEMICAL TREATMENT

The use of a granular insecticide next to the foundation of the house works very well. Treatment of the doorways with a liquid-residual spray labeled for roaches will also help somewhat in keeping these bugs out.

RABBITS

Rabbits are lucky in one very important respect: they're cute. The occasional damage they do to ornamental plants, trees and vegetable gardens is therefore overridden by their darling little wriggling noses, floppy ears and puffy li'l cottontails! Snakes are probably wishing they were this cute; then they wouldn't be slithering away in terror from baseball bats, guns, arrows, skewers, 5-irons, sharp-tipped pencils, and gardening tools.

But I digress. Rabbits are active year-round, usually feeding in the late afternoon and early morning. They eat certain types of vegetation and the stems, bark and buds of woody plants.

The danger of not protecting your garden from these animals is that soon, a few cute rabbits will turn into an invading battalion of wriggling noses, floppy ears and cottontails. Because if there's one thing rabbits do better than almost any other mammal except Wilt Chamberlain, it's reproduce.

Rabbit

Size: 10 to 14 inches long; 1 1/2 to 2 pounds.

IDENTIFICATION & GENERAL INFORMATION

Most rabbits are grey to brown in color with two cute li'l pointy ears, and cute li'l white fluffy tails. Their average litter is around six cute li'l babies. If the weather conditions are good, rabbits can have two cute li'l litters a year!

PREVENTATIVE & LOW-IMPACT TREATMENT

Protect your plants by building out rabbits. Use wire mesh at a height of at least three feet around the entire circumference of your garden. Be sure to bury some of the fence in the ground so the rabbits can't dig under it and devour your veggies.

Removal of rabbit habitat (rabbitat?!) is another good way of controlling these animals. This is best accomplished by clearing your yard of plant debris, heavy vegetation, brush, abandoned machinery, and anything else that may provide rabbit cover.

I was watching a gardening program on TV the other day that recommended a unique way to get rid of rabbits. They said to boil a pound of beef liver, let the water cool, then drain off the liquid and spray it on your plants to discourage rabbits from browsing. Even if the rabbits are scared away, however, every carnivore in the county may be snarling at your fence looking for food in a matter of hours. Try this at your own risk.

Trapping is pretty difficult, too. Even in summer when rabbits are everywhere, these pests are hard to catch. If they're scooting under a fence in your rear yard, put a cage trap there and you may catch Bugs. Once caught, release the critter at least 10 miles away to prevent it from returning.

CHEMICAL TREATMENT

While you can't gas the cute li'l bunnies themselves, you can spray your plants to discourage rabbits from eating them. I've used a product called Ropel with good success on my pansies. Be careful not to be downwind from this spray during use; the bitter taste will last a few days. Kind of like a Pauly Shore movie.

RACCOONS

Pity the species whose best known ancestor was skinned and turned into Davy Crockett's chapeau. Because anyone who has ever encountered one of these smart little buggers knows that they can wreak havoc on your property. With their cunning knack for finding food—even bagged leftovers stuffed in a well-sealed trash can—these sneaky critters can be a homeowner's worst nightmare.

Using their very human-like hands to pry open just about any storage device, these furry garden Houdinis will usually keep at it until they've reached the meal they've sniffed out. Often, they'll even roll back the sod in your lawn in search of grubs and earthworms. Because they're most active at night, raccoons can walk off with half the ripe fruit on your backyard trees before you've even hit REM sleep.

While many other creatures are suffering due to man's encroachment on their natural habitat, these suckers are actually thriving in densely populated suburban neighborhoods. The real danger here is that adults or their young children may find raccoons "cute" and try to play with, or befriend them. In this case, looks are deceiving because raccoons have become the major wildlife host of rabies in the United States. It's the responsibility of parents to properly explain to their young children—and teens—the dangers of any kind of contact with these animals.

Raccoon

Size: 2 to 3 feet long; 10 to 25 pounds.

IDENTIFICATION & GENERAL INFORMATION

This large, stocky mammal is easy to identify by the blackish mask over its eyes and its ringed tail. Their predominant body color is gray mixed with black. Since many raccoons prefer to live near the woods, homes in forested or rural areas tend to have the most problems with them. Being nocturnal, these critters love to open garbage bags when the people of the house are snoozing. In the morning, you can wake to find a big-time 'coon mess waiting for you outside.

Raccoons are strong and during nesting season will rip off wood shingles to enter an attic for shelter. They have even been known to give birth to babies in chimneys.

PREVENTATIVE & LOW-IMPACT TREATMENT

Raccoons can be easily caught in the Tomahawk model 608 live trap, which is 32 x 10 x 12 inches. The best baits include sardines in oil, marshmallows, corn, Cracker Jacks, and chicken bones. When trapping raccoons inside your attic, make sure the trap is on secure flooring. As an added precaution, it's wise to nail the trap down in case the 'coon tries to roll it over.

Also make sure no wires are near the trap. One homeowner was not pleased when a raccoon pulled more than 20 feet of telephone wire into the trap. Maybe he belonged to one of those "Friends and Family" deals.

Always be sure to wear gloves when handling a trapped animal, then seek the assistance of your local animal control department. Do not touch the raccoon's droppings as they contain a large number of parasites. If you just can't help yourself, go talk to a reformed opossum-feces toucher.

CHEMICAL TREATMENT

None

The name "raccoon" comes from the Indian name "aroughcun." Raccoons are omnivorous, meaning they will eat anything they can get their little hands on. Also, contrary to popular belief, raccoons do *not* always wash their food before eating—although they frequently play with their food in water.

RODENTS

Rats would be good in the Olympics. They're strong swimmers, can drop fifty feet without being harmed, and can jump four feet across a flat surface. Plus, they chuck a mean discus. Kidding.

Except for squeaky-voiced Mickey Mouse, rodents aren't really much use to anyone. They attack our homes, offices and vehicles in their incessant search for food. I've known a few people who swear by rats and mice as pets, but I'm not so sure. I really don't want to be sleeping in the same house as anything who might look at my face as an entree, even if it has a cute little pet name.

Many people assume that having a cat around is the most effective way to get rid of rats. Most of the time your cat will just look at this animal as a curiosity and nothing more. Each year in residential areas, cats only kill about one-fifth of the rodent population. In reality, cats and dogs may actually attract rats, which feed on a house pet's food and water.

Getting rid of these unwelcome guests is not an easy job for humans, either. The most effective way to tackle a rodent problem is usually to cut off their food supply and concentrate on barricading your home against them.

Experts estimate that there is at least one rat per person in this country and that each rat can damage or destroy $1,000 worth of food and materials each year.

Beaver

Size: 3 to 5 feet long; 30 to 50 pounds.

IDENTIFICATION & GENERAL INFORMATION

The beaver is the largest rodent in the United States. It is dark brown in color and has a flat, paddle-shaped tail and large webbed feet. Beavers that stay in the wild are great for nature, but it's a different story when they arrive in your yard and wreak havoc on your trees and bushes. Also, contrary to popular belief, the species is not known for its whiny-voiced calls of "Wally!"

PREVENTATIVE & LOW-IMPACT TREATMENT

A number of traps are available, ranging from the leg-type to the large cage-and-suitcase variety. Most of the time, it's easier to hire a professional trapper to solve your problem. However, if you want to attempt it yourself, you'll need a large cage trap. Look in the Yellow Pages under "Trappers," then call and ask if such devices are available in your area.

A humane live trap should measure five feet long, 16 inches high, and 16 inches wide. Fresh-cut saplings or cat-tail roots placed at the back of the trap make good bait. It's essential to place the trap in the area where the beavers are active.

For hard-to-catch beavers, I have used a type of bait known as "beaver castor scent" for more appeal. Once you've trapped a beaver, you'll need to contact your local animal control department and ask where to release the animal. Since beavers are a protected species, make sure you are trapping only the ones that are causing damage to your property.

CHEMICAL TREATMENT

A product is available called Ropel. It is a liquid spray you can apply to tree bark. Ropel's quartenary compounds and bittering agents produce a very bad taste in the mouth of the animal doing the chomping. In many cases, it will convince the beavers to move on to better-tasting quarry. Make sure to treat all trees and shrubs on your property.

Chipmunk

Size: 6 to 8 inches long; 1 1/2 to 3 ounces.

IDENTIFICATION & GENERAL INFORMATION

These small ground rodents are fun to watch, but sometimes can cause damage by burrowing next to the foundation of your home, in your flower beds or on your prized lawn. The holes they make are long, sometimes extending more than 20 feet. Like squirrels, chipmunks can have two litters of young a year, with three to four babies per litter. The chipmunk's preferred diet is nuts and seeds. Chipmunks may look like Chip 'n Dale, but they are not nearly as friendly.

PREVENTATIVE & LOW-IMPACT TREATMENT

Most people prefer getting rid of too-cute-to-kill chipmunks with a live trap. I prefer the Tomahawk 602, which is 16 x 5 x 5 inches. The best bait I have used is a mixture of sunflower seeds and peanut butter. Place the trap near the chipmunk's entrance hole and it should quickly have an occupant. Try to relocate the chipmunk far enough away so it won't return.

Or, just enjoy them and ignore the holes!

CHEMICAL TREATMENT

None

Mouse

Size: 2 to 5 inches long, including the tail.

IDENTIFICATION & GENERAL INFORMATION

These small rodents, gray to dark brown in color, are very good at finding small holes—some just a half-inch wide—where they can gain entry into your home. Most mice get into the kitchen first, then wander up to the attic or down to the basement. The peak periods of mouse activity are the year's coldest months, or when empty fields adjacent to homes are plowed.

Most people who have dogs will see the occasional mouse making a bee-line for poochie's dog food. While they will eat almost anything, mice prefer nuts and grain products. However, they absolutely hate mint. If you can plant some of this stuff in your garden, or in a small pot indoors, you may just drive these tiny, long-tailed garbage disposals elsewhere.

With a home range of 10 to 25 feet from where their nest is, these rodents can be tricky, traveling through the insides of walls in search of grub or to escape predators. However, they give themselves away by whistling like a canary.

Preventative & Low-Impact Treatment

Take preventative measures like storing garbage in sound, smell-proof containers with tight lids. Also, regularly inspect your food-storage areas for signs of infestations, throwing away any packages that may have been penetrated by mice. Never wait too long to clean up a spill of any kind, or else you may find Mighty Mouse lapping it up for you.

Make sure that all entry holes to your house are covered and secure. Discourage mice from living too close to your home by trimming or removing vegetation around foundations and storing firewood and other forms of organic material away from your home.

If, despite your attempts to keep them out, they have invaded your home, all you'll need are six snap traps positioned where you're seeing the mice or their droppings. The best snap trap is one with a wide-trip pan. You'll have a better chance of snaring the mice if you place the traps facing a wall, and fill them with a bait of peanut butter or a ball of cotton.

Another trapping option is glue boards. A single board can

trap up to six mice at once. If you prefer to not kill the mice, humane live traps will catch one critter at a time (Smart Mouse Trap), or as many as 30 in one shot (Victor Tin Cat).

Once caught, you can relocate Mickey and his pals far away from your residence, like to Epcot or something. To avoid getting bit, wear protective clothing, including gloves.

CHEMICAL TREATMENT

If your infestation is especially large, poison baits can be used. I prefer a meal-type bait instead of pellets. Always use tamper-resistant stations to keep non-target animals away from the poison. Mice like to hide under the dishwasher or refrigerator, so these are good places to set the poison. Also, be sure to check the attic, basement and crawl spaces for activity. Always read the labels and make sure that the bait is not accessible to kids and pets.

Norway Rat

Size: 13 to 15 inches long, including the tail; 10 to 17 ounces.

IDENTIFICATION & GENERAL INFORMATION

This very large rat is dark gray in color, but can appear black. Although it's not as good a climber as the roof rat, it is a great swimmer and has been known to enter homes by swimming up through toilets. Quite a shock should you be sitting on the throne.

Norway rats are most active at night. Should you see them during the day, it usually means the population is high, they are sick, or they are very hungry. An omnivore, the Norway rat will eat anything that humans eat.

The home range of this rodent is over 100 feet, meaning they will travel this distance from their nest in search of food. They also tend to stay on the ground or in underground tunnels because they aren't such hot climbers, as I mentioned earlier. The droppings of the Norways are the largest of any rat species, so be prepared to do some serious shoe-scraping if you're not careful.

PREVENTATIVE & LOW-IMPACT TREATMENT

Try to build them out. This rat only needs a one-inch opening to get inside your home, so you have to be vigilant about patching any holes or other entry points. If the Norway rat can squeeze its head in, this persistent rodent can manage to squeeze the rest of its body in behind it.

Don't stack wood next to the house, and trim bushes that would provide a safe haven. If you have outside pets, feed them during the day and bring the food in at night.

When dealing with these "big boys," the most effective weapons are snap traps. Most people prefer to use either the large snap-type traps, or the humane-type cage trap. I prefer the Tomahawk model 602, which is 16 x 5 x 5 inches.

Forget about using glue boards. Most Norway rats are so big they'll hoof right off the boards before you can say, "Whoa, that's a big mother!" I once put a giant glue board out and all I caught was a seven-inch tail. Somewhere in Dallas there is a very large rat with a stump for a tail. And I have an inkling he's pretty mad, too.

CHEMICAL TREATMENT

Poisons can be used. Most rodent baits on the market are called anticoagulants, which means death is caused by internal bleeding.

However, with such a large rodent, the smell of dead rats in the wall can be sickening. Poison baits are easy to use and most of the time the rodent will die outdoors. However, if you want to be sure that there are no dead rats in your walls, use snap or cage traps.

Roof Rat

Size: 15 to 18 inches long, including the tail; 6 to 12 ounces.

IDENTIFICATION & GENERAL INFORMATION

This grayish or dark brown-colored rat is named for its ability to enter homes by climbing up telephone poles, trees and brick walls. Most of the roof rat infestations I've been called out for have been in attics.

The most obvious sign of a roof rat invasion are rat droppings. Those rodents that nest in the attic will head outside at night to feed (they like nuts, dog food, and vegetables), or come down into the house through plumbing voids. Don't seal any holes until the entire rat population has been eradicated.

The roof rat's home range is 100 to 125 feet from where it nests.

PREVENTATIVE & LOW-IMPACT TREATMENT

Use a humane-type cage trap and catch them all at once. The best humane trap I have used is the Tomahawk 602. It's easy to set and the success rate is high. Its size is 16 x 5 x 5 inches.

Most local animal control departments will pick trapped rats up, or you can relocate them. Check with local animal control personnel before you release any rats into your community.

Glue boards will also work in some cases, but get the biggest ones you can find and anchor them down to the rafters with a nail. Once the infestation problem is under control, plug all of the rats' entry areas to prevent reinfestation.

The use of snap traps (the large rat variety) is a good way to pick them off without having them die inside a wall and stinking up the house.

CHEMICAL TREATMENT

If you call a professional, a rodenticide that comes in bags called "toss" packs will likely be used. These are sealed bags of poison that can be tossed to areas where the rats hang out. I have found that most roof rat droppings will be in the attic near the heating unit, so this is a good place to set the baits. Normally, I'll put out at least 10 bags. These "toss" packs can be found at most hardware or pest control stores.

Rats can jump! They can go three feet up and four feet out, from a standing position. With their strong teeth, they can chew through building materials, cinder block, and even glass. They can even climb through pipes with diameters as small as one and one-half inches.

Squirrel

Size: 12 to 18 inches long; 1 1/4 to 2 1/4 pounds

IDENTIFICATION & GENERAL INFORMATION

Most squirrels are gray or dark brown in color. Being good climbers, they are able to enter homes in places people can't easily see. From my experience as a trapper, I find that most squirrels get inside a house at the base of the roof ridge-caps, just above the gutter. Most tree squirrels are active just after sunrise and before sunset, while flying squirrels are liveliest at night.

When they are outside, squirrels are fun to look at. But once they get inside your house, they can cause a lot of damage to wires with their gnawing.

Most species of squirrels can have two litters of young each year—one in the spring and one in the fall. There can be from two to six babies per litter.

PREVENTATIVE & LOW-IMPACT TREATMENT

Live trapping of squirrels that get into your house offers the most effective control. Nuisance squirrels are easy to catch, if you use the right size trap and bait.

Most squirrels are trapped outside the house, rather than in the attic. In some cases, red fox urine can be used to chase them out of confined attic areas. Thinking a predator is near, they will quickly leave.

The best trap that I have used is the Tomahawk model 605 (20 x 7 x 7 inches). This humane trap is easy to set, and allows for easy release of the captured animal with its special sliding rear door.

Look for areas of squirrel activity and place the trap where the animals will see it. I like to put traps on wood fences, roofs, just above a house's gutter, at the base of trees or even on branches. If a squirrel is in an attic, I will place the trap in an area where squirrel activity has been heard. (Be careful when walking in your attic; it can be dangerous).

The best—and tastiest—bait is an apple covered with loganberry paste, with three pecans added for eye appeal. Crunchy peanut butter also works in a pinch.

Once you've trapped the creature, call your local animal control department, or release the squirrels at least 10 miles away. Note: before trapping, check with animal control officials to see if any ordinances apply.

Always use caution and wear protective clothing when handling wild animals. If they are scared, they may scratch or bite you. Kind of like prom dates.

CHEMICAL TREATMENT

None

SCORPIONS

Like most fans of Billy Ray Cyrus, scorpions like to dance before they mate. The male and female face each other and extend their abdomens high into the air. Then they start circling each other slowly, sometimes for days. And you thought your love life was going around in circles!

These pests are also party crashers, with a fondness for invading campsites and especially sleeping bags. You'll know when someone in your group finds a scorpion in their sack because of the new land-speed record they set running the hell out of there. Really, though, they don't have much to worry about. The scorpion's sting, while painful, is rarely fatal to humans. Plus, they sting only when handled or provoked. Of the 75 species of scorpion, just one can inflict a deadly sting.

Only homes located in the scorpions' habitat are at risk of infestation from this pest. Because scorpions can easily slip through holes between bricks or gaps between baseboards, a home's attic will probably be their first stop.

However, life for the picky scorpion will likely be too hot or dry there, so they'll soon invade the home itself, usually terrifying the residents. Since they require water for drinking, scorpions are attracted to the kitchen, bathroom, utility room and air conditioners. Some species, however, can survive up to six months without food or water. Adding to the difficulty of scorpion control is their tendency to hide for two to three months after feeding.

At birth, the young immediately jump onto the mother's back, staying their for about a week. For most species, development to adulthood takes about a year.

Scorpion

Size: 1 to 3 inches long.

IDENTIFICATION & GENERAL INFORMATION

Most scorpions are tan to dark brown in color and are easily recognizable by their pair of large pincers and a segmented tail with a poisonous stinger at the tip. Like women going to a public restroom, it is said that scorpions travel in pairs. So if you find one, its pal probably won't be too far behind.

PREVENTATIVE & LOW-IMPACT TREATMENT

Prevention is the key. Check seals on all doors and try to build the scorpions out. Walk around the house and remove all woodpiles, loose boards and heaps of scattered rock. If you have weep holes around the foundation, stuff copper mesh in them to act as a barrier. Inside the home, glue boards will pick off the stragglers who get past your outside defenses. Most glue boards will last 3 months or longer.

CHEMICAL TREATMENT

Spray the foundation with a micro-encapsulated chemical. Indoor treatment may be needed as well. If scorpions are in the attic, consult a professional exterminator to apply boric acid dust. For do-it-yourselfers, use foggers. Remember to follow all label directions for proper use.

SHREWS

These small critters look a lot like mice, except with longer snouts. Mice also have four-toed front feet and larger eyes. The similarities pretty much end there, especially when a shrew decides to have mouse for dinner. While shrews can become pestiferous by attacking pets, feeding on and contaminating stored foods, or traipsing around your property, they are darn good garden predators, too. Because they feed on beetles, grasshoppers, wasps, crickets, snails, earthworms, butterfly and moth larvae, centipedes and millipedes, shrews can really give you a hand with your garden pest control efforts.

Oh, I forgot one more way you can tell a shrew from a mouse. Shrew feces tends to be corkscrew-shaped. Ain't nature cool?!

Shrew

Size: 1 1/2 to 3 inches long; 1 to 2 ounces.

IDENTIFICATION & GENERAL INFORMATION

This very small mammal, usually dark gray or black in color, is easy to identify by its elongated nose. Shrews are aggressive in their search for food and have been known to attack mice and small birds. Most shrew infestations will occur in basements or garages.

I learned the hard way that their teeth are sharp. When I was a young boy, a shrew bit through one of my gloves and drew blood.

Preventative & Low-Impact Treatment

These animals are only occasional visitors inside homes and buildings. Usually, when a shrew finds itself inside, it will either leave in search of its natural habitat, or die within a couple of days. For those rare recurring shrew visits, snap-type mouse traps and glue boards will catch a persistent pest. Since shrews eat insects, gluing a cricket to the trip pan works well.

Chemical Treatment

Currently, no toxicants are registered to poison shrews. Also, since shrews are not grain feeders, rodent poisons generally won't work either.

SILVERFISH

Believe it or not, silverfish have actually been around longer than the cockroach. An unlucky thirteen species of this common household insect have been recorded in the United States, including the common silverfish and the firebrat. The former is named for its shining gray color and pattern of movement; the latter for its brown color. Outdoors, silverfish are commonly found under rocks, bark, logs, in leaf litter, and in the nests of animals and birds. While not much of a danger to humans, they can cause damage to fabric and paper products. These "bookworms" like to munch on your favorite reading material. Unable to climb slick porcelain surfaces, they also can get trapped in sinks and bathtubs.

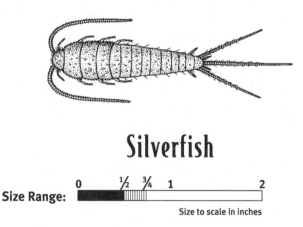

Silverfish

Size Range:

| 0 | ½ | ¾ | 1 | | | 2 |

Size to scale in inches

IDENTIFICATION & GENERAL INFORMATION

This insect is easily recognized by its elongated, carrot-shaped body. Three tail projections can be found at the rear of the insect, with two long antennae at the front. When you touch a silverfish, grayish scales easily come off on your fingers.

Silverfish and firebrats can live up to seven years—a long time in insect years—but high humidity is required for survival. This is why bathrooms, kitchens, attics, and crawl spaces are often their residences of choice. The higher the number of these pests you find, the older the infestation.

PREVENTATIVE & LOW-IMPACT TREATMENT

Cut them off before they can get inside by closing off any holes around pipes at their point of entry to the wall. Also, repair any plumbing leaks immediately, thereby eliminating a valuable source of water for the silverfish.

Back inside the house, try to clean out your bookcases once in a while, shaking out each volume to dislodge any silverfish that may be happily munching on your poetry or prose. If you like to collect old books, check each new purchase carefully for signs of silverfish infestation.

CHEMICAL TREATMENT

Apply an approved liquid-residual spray to cracks and crevices of baseboards. These pests like to hide in dark places, so move furniture and treat the area behind it. Be sure to get to the source of the problem—wall voids and attics. Attics, the source for most silverfish infestation, can be dusted with boric acid powder or fogged with pyrethrum. Plan your attack at the beginning of each spring and fall.

Plumbing voids can be dusted with boric acid or a DE/pyrethrum mixture. Be sure to wear a paper mask when dusting. Spot application to infested areas with a liquid synthetic pyrethroid should also prove successful.

SKUNKS

I used to be under the misconception that all skunks had was one good shot of stink, but early in my trapping career I was hit by second and third discharges. Needless to say, my wife made me sleep on the couch that night.

If your clothes or some other object of yours gets blasted by skunk juice, there are a few things you can use to get the smell out. Tomato juice and vinegar diluted with water will help to treat items tainted by the distinctive mark of the skunk. A brand new recipe for skunk odor removal is one quart hydrogen peroxide, one-quarter cup baking soda, and one teaspoon liquid soap. Use only enough for what you will need. Do not store in any glass container. When put onto clothes, the mixture will foam; then simply rinse with clear, cool water. Remember to wear gloves! And test the mixture first on an inconspicuous piece of the garment to make sure it doesn't stain.

While their odor may be their most famous offense, skunks can also cause damage by digging under foundations and living beneath homes or other buildings. They're also second to raccoons in the number of rabies cases caused in the United States.

Skunk

Size: 1 1/2 to 2 feet long; 3 to 10 pounds.

Identification & General Information

This stinky pest is a member of the weasel family, and is disliked primarily for the reason I mentioned: it makes stuff stink real bad. However, these animals will only discharge an odor as a self-defense mechanism when provoked. Two internal glands near the base of the tail produce the thick, oily liquid that contains enough sulfur compounds to make you pray for a sinus cold. Skunks will usually stamp their front feet rapidly, hiss, growl, or walk on their front feet with their tail erect as a warning before releasing their scent. Come to think of it, I knew a guy in college who had the same ritual after eating cheap Mexican food.

Preventative & Low-Impact Treatment

If they are "denning" under your house or deck, the only option is to live-trap them. The ideal trap is the Tomahawk model 606 (26 x 9 x 9 inches). The best baits I have used are sardines in oil, bananas, raw eggs or cooked bacon.

Once the skunks are caught, keep children and family pets away from them. Wrapping the trap with a plastic bag poked with air holes will calm the skunk down, making it less likely to spray. Call your local animal control department for proper disposal instructions.

Chemical Treatment

None

SNAILS AND SLUGS

Slugs are basically snails without shells. Apparently, slugs are jealous, because they seem to be a lot meaner. While a few species of snails are considered pestiferous, slugs are much more damaging to your garden.

These two soft-bodied mollusks are found in every region of the United States. They prefer foggy, rainy climates, which provide them with the life-sustaining water that they absorb through their skin or drink from puddles. The snail or slug's body is 80 percent water; its slime is 98 percent water.

During daylight hours, they normally hide under stones or thick ground cover, but might be found looking for food in garbage cans. Once they find a hiding place, they usually return often, only emerging at night or during warm, damp weather.

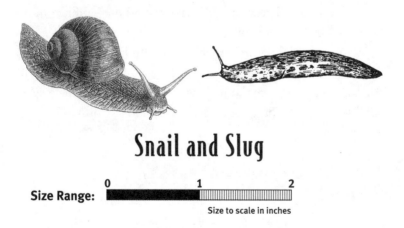

Snail and Slug

| Size Range: | 0 | 1 | 2 |

Size to scale in inches

IDENTIFICATION & GENERAL INFORMATION

Slugs can be as colorful as a rainbow. Most of these critters are pale brown, some purple, or lavender, or even black with brown specks. Maybe because God has already chosen their outerwear, snails are much less varied in tone.

The best time to begin looking for slugs and snails is in the early spring. Warning signs include sizable and ragged holes in leaves, fruits, stems and slime trails on leaves or soil.

While snails stick to greens in their diet, slugs will eat almost anything, although they do have a preference for damaged plants and rotting leaves, usually attacking the plant parts closest to the ground first. Inside your home, if you discover a slimy trail on your carpet or tile in the morning, it probably was created by a slug or snail. Or else your kid forgot to use Kleenex again.

Preventative & Low-Impact Treatment

Mulch sometimes makes snail and slug problems worse because they tend to be moist. If you're having a problem with these slimers, remove mulch until the infestation is controlled.

Diversifying vegetation and groundcover will also attract a wide range of slug and snail predators, including toads, snakes, and salamanders. While you're at it, plant some wormwood and rosemary. Snails and slugs sniff or nibble these herbs and immediately volunteer at Escargots-R-Us.

Special slug traps made of plastic can also be placed below the surface of the ground. Beer is added and the slug drowns— but has a darn good time doing it! If you pour salt on visible slugs, they will die quickly. Snails will most likely not survive the clomp of a heavy boot on their brittle shells.

You can even pluck slugs and snails off plants if you see them. Don't worry, they don't bite.

Chemical Treatment

A bait containing the active ingredient metaldehyde or mesurol is recommended. Most formulations are pellet-hard and used outdoors. When the pellets get wet, they swell up and the slug will eat it. Be careful, however, that children or pets don't come in contact with the bait, because it can be very dangerous.

SNAKES

M ost snakes are useful because of the rodents and insects that they the devour. Some actually eat other snakes. Snakes (with the exception of the racer snake) will not charge or attack humans, unless they are cornered. Then they will react in one of many ways: playing dead, hissing, opening their mouth in a threatening manner, or coiling and striking. They bite only when necessary.

Of the 116 species of snakes found in the United States, only 19 are dangerous. Fifteen of them are rattlesnakes, two are moccasins, and two are coral snakes. So that doesn't leave much else for people to get all worked up about. But, alas, few reptiles frighten people more. In fact, many people kill a snake before identifying what variety it is. That's like shooting the first stranger that rings your doorbell, then realizing it was the Domino's guy.

For creatures without legs, snakes can move surprisingly fast. They do this by employing four types of locomotion. The most common manner is a simple crawl known as the serpentine method. Desert snakes use the sidewinding method, in which the body rolls sidewise in a looping motion. Heavy-bodied snakes use the caterpillar method, which moves them along in a straight line. The concertina method, allowing the body to alternately stretch out and pull together, is used in climbing. The fastest speed any snake can travel is 8 m.p.h., slower than the average person can run.

Snake

Size: 1 to 5 feet long.

IDENTIFICATION & GENERAL INFORMATION

There are two types of snakes in the United States: those that are harmless and those that are poisonous. Most snakes that you will encounter are harmless. The easiest way to tell if a snake is lethal is by looking at its head.

Poisonous snakes will have a head somewhat triangular in shape, and elliptical pupils. Non-poisonous snakes will have narrow-shaped heads and round pupils. Be sure you get this designation down cold or else the last thing you do on earth may be making friendly goo-goo talk to a slithering assassin.

If you are outside and can't determine which variety of snake you have encountered, leave it alone and get away as fast as you can.

PREVENTATIVE & LOW-IMPACT TREATMENT

If you live in snake country, exclusion is the best remedy. Trim the bushes next to your home and remove all woodpiles that touch the house. Keep the grass cut short. Snakes are helpful to nature, so try not to kill them. If you cannot trap and release a snake that gets inside your home, contact the local animal control department.

In the unlikely event that you do find a snake inside your home, you can also use glue boards. I use the Catchmaster rat-size version. Apply cooking oil to the glue, which will help the snake to wiggle free after it's removed from the home.

Snap traps can also be effective. Try professional rat traps that have wide-trip pans. Place two or three of the traps along the wall. There is no need to use bait.

Snake grabbers are poles that have a grip handle and end tongs for grabbing a snake. Once you have the snake, it cannot get loose. The grabbers come in various lengths, from two to six feet.

CHEMICAL TREATMENT

You can use Dr. T's Snake-A-Way (active ingredient: sulfur and naphthalene), a repellent that is available in stores. It is a pelletized product intended for use around the outside foundation of your home. Snakes do not like the smell of it and stay away from treated areas. Information is sketchy whether this product also works on Amway salesmen.

Movie Review

Arachnophobia (1990) — Yawn... A whole heap of potentially dangerous spiders infest some guy's suburban home, forcing him to call out a pest control operator. Welcome to my Mondays, kids. Aside from the fact that a native South American spider would have a difficult time assimilating in this made-up town's environment, I had some problems with John Goodman's exterminator character. Stereotyping pest control professionals as fat, weird freaks doesn't really go over well at my house, let me tell you. Plus, the movie was just plain boring.

 (All reviews are on a scale of 1 to 5 roaches, with 5 being best.)

SPIDERS

There are countless tales of how spiders have inspired humankind. In the fourteenth century, for example, Robert the Bruce faced sure defeat in his war with the British. He gained new confidence while watching a spider slowly and patiently weave its web and Bruce was able to ultimately march to victory. Sadly, the spider was felled by a spear as he bravely charged the enemy line.

Spiders are our allies not just in war, but also in the garden. You need as many as possible, since they feed primarily on insects which can damage your plants and flowers. Inside our homes, spiders are, for the most part, harmless. With the exception of the black widow, brown recluse, and tarantula, these multi-legged crawlers are threats to us in our minds alone.

Certain large spiders, however, are strong enough to kill small birds, fish, and rats. All spiders use their poison glands to capture prey, but their jaws are usually too small and weak to pierce human skin.

Even with the eight eyes common for most species of spiders, these insects can only see clearly for just a few inches. However, their sense of hearing and touch is excellent. A few species of spiders are even able to produce sounds.

Male spiders are fewer in number, smaller in size, and generally more brightly colored than the females.

Black Widow Spider

Size Range:

```
0              1    1½  1¾  2
■■■■■■■■■■■■■■■      ▥▥▥▥
```

Size to scale in inches

IDENTIFICATION & GENERAL INFORMATION

The female is easy to recognize by her jet black color and red, hourglass-shaped marking on her underbelly. The male is brownish in color and much smaller in size.

As mentioned above, the black widow is one of the very few species of poisonous spider. Its venom is a neurotoxin. If bitten, seek immediate medical attention and bring the spider, if possible, for proper identification. Most hospitals will have antitoxins on hand to counteract the effect of the spider poison.

This spider rarely comes indoors. Most of the time, it stays close to a house's foundation, on a fence, or at a corner garage entrance.

PREVENTATIVE & LOW-IMPACT TREATMENT

Remove outdoor cover favored by these spiders like old bricks and concrete blocks, loose bark, logs and other seldom disturbed debris. Also, store woodpiles a good distance from your house's foundation. If any article of clothing or play item has been left outdoors or in the garage for an extended period, be sure to inspect them closely for spiders before bringing them into the house. Many poisonous bites result from spiders hiding in clothing, shoes or other harborages.

Another preventative measure is the use of a glue board in the corners of the garage, near the entrance. This way, you can catch the black widows before they have time to build a nest.

CHEMICAL TREATMENT

A spot application of pyrethrum will quickly kill this spider. The dusting of weep holes and cracks and crevices with a residual dust will also help to prevent an infestation.

Since you will typically encounter no more than one or two black widows in one place at one time, the use of a residual spray applied directly to the spider will also do the job. Most of the time, black widows stay in their nest and will be easy to spray. If you live in the country or a new subdivision, apply a preventative spraying to your home's foundation.

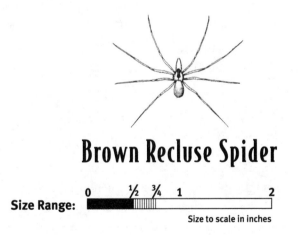

Brown Recluse Spider

Size Range:

0   ½ ¾ 1   2

Size to scale in inches

IDENTIFICATION & GENERAL INFORMATION

This is one of the most dangerous spiders in the United States. Its color can vary from dark brown to light brown. The brown recluse is frequently called the "fiddleback" or "violin spider" because of the violin-shaped mark on the top of its back, just behind the head.

This species is known as the brown recluse because it lives in dark, secluded areas such as closets and attics. It can also be found behind furniture that is rarely moved. Of the infestations I've seen, most have been in attics and garages.

The brown recluse is most active at night, and is indeed a very dangerous spider. Approach it with extreme caution.

PREVENTATIVE & LOW-IMPACT TREATMENT

Prior to conducting any type of treatment, it is important to do a thorough cleaning of the house and garage. Eliminate clutter in closets, attics, basements and garages by disposing of old boxes, unused clothing or playthings, baskets, buckets or anything else that may say "Home Sweet Home" to a wandering spider. Vacuum weekly under beds and behind furniture.

In some cases, I've been able to control these spiders by placing boards under all the furniture, as well as in the attic and garage. Also remove potential outdoor hiding places like wood debris, or loose bricks and concrete blocks just laying there on the ground. Wear gloves during the cleaning process.

CHEMICAL TREATMENT

Use a good liquid-residual spray on spot areas of the baseboards, as well as along cracks and crevices inside the house. In the attic, use a good residual-type fogger. If you think your infestation is particularly severe, hire a professional to dust the attic.

The use of a pyrethrum fogger in the attic would also be beneficial. A number of applications may be needed to control this persistent pest. Make sure all pilot lights are off.

Tarantula

Size: 4 to 5 inches long.

IDENTIFICATION & GENERAL INFORMATION

This very large spider, known as "nature's exterminator," is mostly brown or black in color. When seen, it is usually crawling around a yard, in a garage, or crossing a road. Sometimes, when it's approached, the tarantula will stand on its rear legs in an attempt to scare the intruder away. If that doesn't work, the spider will start humming tunes from *Cats*. Both of these defenses are usually effective.

The tarantula has a pair of poison fangs, but unless you grab the critter, it won't bite you.

PREVENTATIVE & LOW-IMPACT TREATMENT

Leave the ones outside alone to eat your bugs. Should tarantulas get inside, however, use the heal of your shoe or a broom to scoot them back to the yard. You can also try to catch them, then let them go.

Glue boards also work well as a non-chemical approach.

CHEMICAL TREATMENT

Spray a micro-encapsulated chemical mixture around the foundation of your home. However, you should only utilize this preventative measure when you feel tarantulas have become a problem on your property. If undisturbed, these spiders pose no harm to you.

SPRINGTAILS

$\int$ pringtails are found in areas that are wet or humid. I've spotted them near potted plants, in sinks and outside on the ground near entrances to houses. Their food of choice is high organic matter (leaf litter, grass clippings, etc.) and fungi.

Because they jump around like spit on a griddle, these bugs are often thought to be fleas. But nothing could be farther from the truth. Springtails will go hog-wild in a garbage bin, but start scribbling suicide notes if they're forced to spend all day stuck on a dog's back.

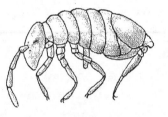

Springtail

Size: 1/16 inch long.

IDENTIFICATION & GENERAL INFORMATION

This whitish-colored insect's flea-like characteristics are limited to an expert skill at jumping. Under low magnification, you can see the bug's humped back and forked tail that allows it to spring forward.

PREVENTATIVE & LOW-IMPACT TREATMENT

In general, you should try to eliminate as much moisture as possible from your home and garden.

If you see springtails in the sink, cover about 90 percent of the drain with masking tape, then don't use the sink for a few days. The tape should catch most of them. Remove any potted plants in the area.

CHEMICAL TREATMENT

The use of an approved insecticide spray will knock the adults out very quickly. Make spot applications to the areas in the yard where you see this pest. The area next to the foundation, under the windows, is the key treatment area.

If you have a lot of potted plants, treat the soil with a pyrethrum-based plant spray. The best one I have used is Schultz-Instant insect spray.

TERMITES

Despite their diminutive size, there is nothing small about termite statistics. As many as one million insects may inhabit a single colony. It should go without saying, therefore, that these little pests are prodigious breeders. In certain tropical species, the queen grows to hundreds or even thousands of times the size of the worker—her abdomen so full of eggs that she can't even move. In other species, the female lays upwards of 30,000 eggs in a single day. And you thought your last delivery was difficult!

Most homeowners only see termites when they swarm out of walls via a mud launching pad somewhere in a house's plumbing. Swarmers do no damage; their main purpose is to mate and start another colony. It's the workers, located behind the walls, that do all of the damage.

Each year in the United States, more than 300,000 homes are treated for termites. But unless you live in a warm climate, you may never have seen these insects. Allow me to clarify. Termites, often confused with the winged ant, fall into two categories: subterranean, which thrive in the ground, and non-subterranean, which subsist on the wood they infest.

Subterranean termites are the biggest trouble-causers and typically reside in moist soils. They then dig their way to wood sources to obtain food. Left alone, they will eat the wood until nothing remains except a shell. Fortunately, it takes termites a long time to inflict this kind of severe damage.

That gives you time to find out what your options are. Your first step should always be to determine if an active termite infestation exists. The presence of swarmers or their shed wings almost always indicates a termite infestation. However, most times, termite colonies will not be outwardly visible to you without taking a flashlight into crawl spaces and other potential trouble spots. The most telling feature of subterranean termite damage is the presence of a brown mud-like gunk lining the insides of your walls in irregular patterns. You can also tap on the wall that you think may be infested and listen for the hollow sound of damaged wood.

If you suspect that your home or property is, in fact, suffering an invasion of these stubborn pests, immediate action should be taken. As mentioned earlier in this book, I highly recommend calling a professional to eradicate your termite problem.

Slab homes will usually have to be drilled and a pressurized chemical pumped in to form barriers that prevent termite entry. In other types of homes (pier and beam), trenches are made and then all piers and the foundation are treated. Dirt-filled porches and expansion joints of the garage are drilled and treated with a chemical residual. Chemical barriers are placed under a house and around it. This won't eradicate the entire colony, just those termites from the treated ground on up. Termites return to the colony every 24 to 48 hours. They die if a barrier is established and they can't get back to the ground.

New to the market are baiting systems. See a professional for details.

In Singapore, for the equivalent of seven dollars, you can have a prime 2-inch long termite queen for dinner. Locals believe this will improve one's health.

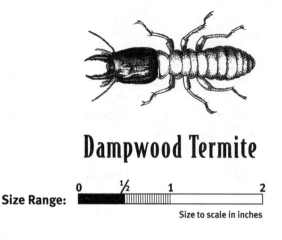

Dampwood Termite

Size Range:

0   ½   1   2

Size to scale in inches

IDENTIFICATION & GENERAL INFORMATION

This large termite is usually found in damp or rotten wood. Unlike subterranean termites that must make contact with soil in order to survive, the dampwood termite can live above ground with no soil contact.

The fecal pellets of this termite will be found in areas of high activity, either on window sills or carpet. The adults are amber-colored, while nymphs are a cream color. This species swarms at night during the spring and can cause very extensive damage.

PREVENTATIVE & LOW-IMPACT TREATMENT

The best way of controlling termites is keeping them out of your house in the first place. Remove any wooden debris that may become a source of infestation beneath your house. This includes scrap wood, form boards, old tree roots and even sawdust! Outside, eliminate any infested stumps or trees close to your foundation.

If this species gains access to your wall voids, you can ensure that there's not enough moisture for them to survive by reducing humidity through cross-ventilation. Draping the ground with roofing paper will also cut down on sub-structural humidity by lessening soil evaporation.

CHEMICAL TREATMENT

Before new home construction, it's a good idea to have all wood treated with a boron-based product, such as Bora-Care or Tim-Bor. Contact a professional pest control specialist; this job is not for the do-it-yourselfer.

If an invasion of these pests occurs in a mature home, contact a local pest control company, which may have to tarp and fumigate your house, as well as treat the soil.

Nearly five hundred homes could be built with the amount of wood that termites chew up in an average year.

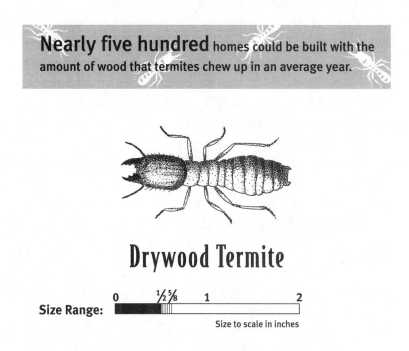

Drywood Termite

Size Range:

0   ½ ⅝   1   2

Size to scale in inches

IDENTIFICATION & GENERAL INFORMATION

This large species is yellowish-brown in color. Swarming takes place at night in the spring. The drywood termite doesn't need soil contact and can infest wood with a low moisture content. As a result, most drywood termite problems are in coastal and subtropical areas of the United States. The majority of infestations are easy to spot because of the fecal pellets that are expelled. Major structural damage can be caused by this voracious termite.

PREVENTATIVE & LOW-IMPACT TREATMENT

Believe it or not, termite-infested telephone and electrical poles may lead to an infestation of your house as well. If these diseased wood pilings are upwind from your home, flying drywood termites may be able to soar right on over to your place. Try to arrange for your local utility company to remove these infested poles before they cause termite problems for the whole neighborhood.

Another way to keep the flying drywoods out of your house is by screening all vents—including those in eaves, attics, walls and crawl spaces—with virtually impenetrable 20-mesh non-corroding metal screening. This way, the reproductives will be treated to a screen sandwich when they try to fly into your home. Check your local building codes first.

The use of heat is now being tried to kill termites. With special equipment, rooms are heated to 150 degrees Fahrenheit for a short period of time.

CHEMICAL TREATMENT

Before structures can be treated, they must be tented and fumigated. This should be done only by a highly trained pest control specialist. Not too many companies are equipped for this work, so consult your phone book.

The largest termite mound was found in Australia. It was 20 feet high and 34 feet wide at the base. The tallest mound ever recorded belonged to an African species, measuring forty-two and one-half feet (and less than 10 feet wide at the base).

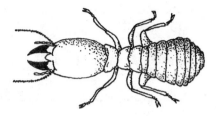

Eastern Subterranean Termite

Size Range:

0   1/4 3/8   1   2

Size to scale in inches

IDENTIFICATION & GENERAL INFORMATION

Most homeowners see termites when they come swarming out of the walls via a mud launching pad in the plumbing area of the house. Swarmers do no damage; their main purpose is to mate and start another colony. The workers, located behind the walls, do all of the damage. Termites have special protozoa in their stomachs that allow them to digest cellulose found in paper and wood. In Texas we have a saying: there are two types of homes, those that have termites and those that will get termites.

PREVENTATIVE & LOW-IMPACT TREATMENT

A number of termite baits are on the market, including Sentricon and First Line (which should be applied by a professional pest control operator). When your house is treated with these products, bait stations are placed on the ground. The termites will take the product back to the colony and they will be wiped out. I think that baiting will be the treatment of choice in the future, but more research needs to be done in this area.

CHEMICAL TREATMENT

In most cases, eradicating termites is not for do-it-your-selfers. Slab homes usually have to be drilled and a chemical is pumped in under pressure to form barriers that prevent termite entry. In other types of homes (pier and beam), drenches next to all piers and the foundation must be dug and then treated. The chemical barrier is put under the house and around it. The entire termite colony is not killed—just those termites from the treated ground upwards. Termites return to the colony every 24 to 48 hours. They die if a barrier is established and they can't get back to the ground.

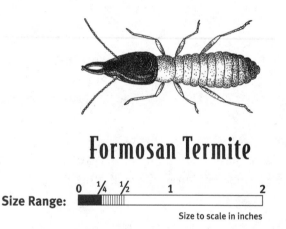

Formosan Termite

Size Range: 0   ¼ ½   1   2

Size to scale in inches

IDENTIFICATION & GENERAL INFORMATION

This termite is pale yellow, but at times can be yellowish-brown. The workers are identified by their oval-shaped head and their jaws, which cross at the tips.

Because they live in large colonies, Formosan termites can cause a lot of damage in a short period of time. As a subterranean species, Formosans must make contact with moist soil to survive. Therefore, most swarming is done at night after a heavy spring rain. Very aggressive termites and a queen can lay over 1,000 eggs per day.

PREVENTATIVE & LOW-IMPACT TREATMENT

First, try to eliminate all wood contact with the ground. This can be done by replacing wooden posts and pilings with concrete varieties, or supporting wooden steps on a concrete base. If these subterranean pests can't get to the wood, they can't infest it.

Also, fill any crevices or voids where Formosans can move from the ground to wood in buildings. These areas include foundation cracks, hollow blocks, gaps between wall and stucco, and openings around pipework.

CHEMICAL TREATMENT

Pre-treat wood with boron-based products such as Bora-Care or Tim-Bor. Contact your local pest control specialist for details, or to set up a consultation.

If you do have a Formosan termite infestation, eradicating it is a job for a professional, not a do-it-yourselfer. Contact your local termite company for more information. Treatment to the ground as well as fumigation may be needed.

One queen termite can live to the ripe old age of 70, laying as many as eighty thousand eggs *a day* in her fertilization period. The workers and soldiers of the colony are blind and live only two to five years.

THRIPS

To the naked eye, these tiny insects look like miniature grand prix courses, all squiggly and curvy. But the similarity ends there. You won't find a grand prix course eating up your plants, or feeding on mites or small aphids. Plus, you probably couldn't fit a Formula One car on a thrip to save your life.

These pests seem to do best under dry conditions, so will likely not be found in the rainy Pacific Northwest, or other dampness prone areas.

When attacking foliage, thrips scratch at the surface of plant tissue, then suck up the resulting juice. Sometimes, the damage isn't obvious, because they do their scratching and sucking on the underside of leaves, near the veins. But eventually the infested leaf will become discolored and disfigured, and finally dry up.

While thrips will feed on leaves, fruits and flowers, they seem especially fond of light-colored flowers. Well, I guess now you know what to get that special thrip on your anniversary.

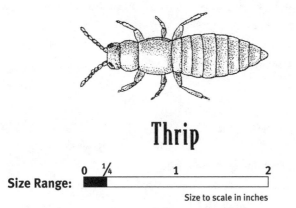

Thrip

| Size Range: | 0 | ¼ | 1 | 2 |

Size to scale in inches

IDENTIFICATION & GENERAL INFORMATION

You'll probably have a hard time seeing thrips with your naked eye. They can be either pale or dark, and are very narrow. Sometimes, the only way to determine if you have a thrip infestation is by shaking a flower over white paper and looking for the thrip larvae, or their fecal pellets (small, dark-colored specks).

Of the six stages of a thrip's life cycle, only the larval and adult stages do any damage to plants. Adults can fly, but the larvae cannot.

PREVENTATIVE & LOW-IMPACT TREATMENT

Some plant varieties are more thrip-resistant than others. For example, many types of cabbage can still thrive with thrips sucking their juices night and day. Talk to someone at your local garden store to find out which plant species in your area can best survive thrip infestations.

Also, try to keep the vegetation around your garden diverse to attract one of the many natural enemies of the thrip. Misting your plants during dry weather will also help to ward off these pests, who do their best work in arid conditions.

For thrips that pupate in the soil, cover them with paper, plastic, or other impermeable mulches to help prevent the adults from emerging later.

CHEMICAL TREATMENT

First off, make sure to only spray infested plants at the locus of thrip activity, and only attack thrip species that feed on leaves. For woody plants, spray a superior light horticultural oil over the entire plant. If it is specifically the foliage being attacked, spray an insecticidal soap on the underside of infested leaves every four or five days for a period of two weeks. Remember to always wear a mask when using these products. Read label for temperature ratings when using this product.

TICKS

Ticks can transmit more diseases to humans than any other arthropod, with the exception of mosquitoes. Usually not a problem for city dwellers, ticks are mostly found in wilderness areas, mountains, forests, and areas with thick vegetation.

Ticks belong to one of two groups: soft ticks or hard ticks. The former lay several small clutches of eggs, while the latter deposit eggs in one large clutch, typically containing several thousand eggs.

Ticks have four developmental stages: egg, six-legged larva, eight-legged nymph, and adult. Adult ticks like to hang on blades of grass, wood fences, and tree trunks, making it easy to attach themselves to dogs. Most ticks can live up to two years.

Usually, tick problems in your home begin with your pet. Cats, possibly because they lick themselves so much, rarely get ticks. Dogs are another story. The adult parasite can generally be found on a dog's ears, neck, and between its toes. Young adults (larvae and nymphs) prefer the long hairs along the dog's back. The loss of blood from a tick infestation can cause severe weakness in a dog.

There are novel ways to remove ticks from humans, including the adhesive tape method. In this technique, fresh tape is applied to the infested area, as long as the tick isn't swollen. It is believed that the chemicals in the adhesive irritate or suffocate the tick. When the tape is removed the next day, the tick will come off with it.

An effective, but less than practical, preventative measure is not to bathe for an extended period of time. Ticks will stay away from you, but so will your family and friends. I guess you have to determine which are the bigger pests. In any case, you should check with your doctor before trying to remove a tick yourself.

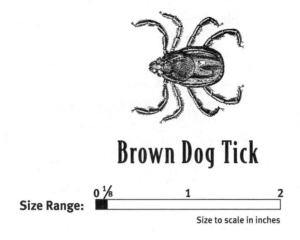

Brown Dog Tick

Size Range:

0 ⅛   1   2

Size to scale in inches

IDENTIFICATION & GENERAL INFORMATION

This tick is oval-shaped and mostly chestnut brown in color, with a white patch on its head. After the female takes a blood meal, she will swell up to about 1/2 inch long.

PREVENTATIVE & LOW-IMPACT TREATMENT

Prevention is your best defense. After returning from a walk with your dog, inspect the animal closely for ticks. When the parasites first attach themselves, they're much easier to remove and have little time for disease transmission.

You should also closely trim your lawn and shrubs so that ticks and their rodent hosts have no places to hide on your property. When you go hiking or walking in rural, woodsy areas, wear sturdy pants, secure boots, and a long-sleeved shirt to prevent the critters from hitching a ride on you.

CHEMICAL TREATMENT

The yard should be treated with a liquid-residual spray using a hose-end sprayer. Prior to treatment of your yard, cut the grass.

Then be sure to treat all grass areas, as well as wood fences and tree trunks.

If you have a doghouse, treat it as well. Several applications may be required. And if you treat the house, you might as well treat the dog, too. They should be dipped and inspected religiously for ticks.

Most of the time, treatment will be limited to the yard and dog only. But in some cases, the house foundation, wood fences and trees should be treated from one to three feet above the ground.

Deer Tick

Size: 1/16 to 1/18 inch long.

IDENTIFICATION & GENERAL INFORMATION

Reddish in color, deer ticks prefer to infest wild deer and the white-footed mouse. They are infamous for carrying the dreaded Lyme disease.

PREVENTATIVE & LOW-IMPACT TREATMENT

Prevention is a major part of controlling this pest. Keep the area outside your home as tidy as possible. This will help to keep away the white-footed mice that may house deer ticks. Also, screen or seal openings which may allow entry of potentially infested rodents.

As birds can also be carriers of these ticks, you should discourage nesting or roosting on your building using anti-roosting devices, and also by removing old nests. Rodents also play an important part in the life cycle of a tick; make sure to eradicate these pests if they appear in or around your house.

CHEMICAL TREATMENT

When in deer country, you should wear an insect repellent. Look for products that have either DEET or permethrin as the active ingredient. Make sure to thoroughly check your body for ticks upon returning from the field. Always check with your doctor before trying to remove a tick from your body yourself.

If you live in an area of the country where this tick is common, treat the lower foundation of your house with a micro-encapsulated chemical as a preventative measure.

WHITEFLIES

D espite their name, whiteflies are not flies at all, but rather plant-sucking bugs related to aphids and mealybugs. Whitefly-infest-ed plants are pretty easy to spot: they usually have wispy filaments of white stuff clustered on their leaves that look like vanilla cotton candy. Unfortunately, it's not so tasty for the diseased plant. These pests are primarily attracted to yellowish green plant parts, which usually means the young—and very vulnerable—stem ends and newly formed leaves.

The female whitefly lays her eggs on the underside of mature leaves. The eggs hang from the leave by a short stalk, then hatch into mobile larvae that start sucking plant juices. Larvae pupate and develop a cocoonlike protective cover (the cotton candy) that lets them suck in peace.

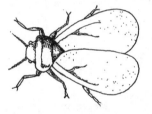

Whitefly

Size: 1/16 to 1/8 inch long (larvae are almost microscopic).

IDENTIFICATION & GENERAL INFORMATION

The adults look like—duh!—little white flies. You'll see them swarming around an infested leaf or plant. When disturbed, the whiteflies will likely swarm in a cloud, then head straight back to a plant's youngest foliage. They don't fly off very far, except if caught in a strong wind gust or the high-pressure stream of a garden hose.

Whitefly eggs will usually be laid in a small circle and look like greenish tubes dangling below a leaf. When they hatch into larvae, they become translucent little spots, moseying around young plant growth while looking for juice to suck.

PREVENTATIVE & LOW-IMPACT TREATMENT

Put on a glove and wipe the larvae and pupae off the plant gently, without damaging the young leaves or stems. If it's early in the season when whitefly populations are low, you can even use a hand-vac to suck the adults off the leaves. The best time for fly sucking is in the morning, when the critters are sluggish.

Yellow sticky traps work well to trap the airborne whiteflies. In a pinch, spraying the leaves with soapy water will get the bugs off temporarily. But remember, it's not the adults that damage the plants, but the juice-slurping larvae.

Some species of herb can also discourage whiteflies from hanging around. So if you've got an herb garden, try including some nicandra, marigold and nasturtium. Whiteflies hate these plants like the plague.

CHEMICAL TREATMENT

Insecticidal soaps or light horticultural oils can be sprayed on the undersides of affected leaves. But make sure only older, more mature leaves are sprayed, and that the foliage contains larvae and pupae infestations. You can also spray the flying adults directly if you're having a bad day and want to see something die and plummet to the earth. Read and follow all label directions carefully.

DO-IT-YOURSELF CHECKLIST

Caulking Equipment: This can be either a caulking gun or tube with a tapered applicator end. These are used to seal cracks and crevices that may provide pest entry into your home, or a specific room.

Copper Mesh: Available at hardware stores, this material is good for closing off openings in walls, foundations or fences where pests can enter.

Crack and Crevice Applicator: These applicators guide paste baits and gel baits into tight spaces using syringe-style cartridges. Crack and crevice extension tubes nozzles are also available for attachment to pumps and sprayers to apply pesticides into narrow target areas.

Eyeshields: You need to make sure your eyes are protected from the potentially noxious sprays and mists used to eliminate certain pests.

Flashlight: Possibly the most important pest-management device, the flashlight illuminates the often pitch-dark attics, basements and crawl spaces—in addition to nooks and crannies in storage areas—where pests often hide.

Hand Duster: This is used to introduce thin layers of pesticide dust into cracks and crevices and various cabinet wall or equipment voids.

Ice Pick: Use this to make small openings in Sheetrock to inject products into wall voids.

Magnifier: A magnifier that increases the size of your bugs by 15 to 30 times will help you to identify the pest.

Moisture Meter: A nice tool to have around when hunting for dampness-loving pests, this device can pinpoint moisture problems that may be the cause of insect infestations or structural deficiencies in wood.

Particle Mask: This keeps you from breathing such dusts as DE or boric acid dust.

Rubber Gloves: Because you will be handling chemical products, it's a must to keep your hands covered at all times.

Sprayers: Whether they're hand-pumped models or large hydraulic machines, sprayers usually consist of a tank, a pressurization device, a delivery line to the valve, and another line from the valve to a nozzle.

Screwdriver: Handy when you need to open a vent, or remove some other screw-tightened cover.

GLOSSARY OF INSECTICIDES AND PEST CONTROL TERMS

Aerosols: A pressurized can that emits a fine spray of chemicals. A good example would be the product Raid.

Attractants: Products that attract the pests we are trying to control to enter a trap or to eat a poison. Most attractants will be food grade material or pheromones.

Bacillus Thuringiensis (BT): This is a species of live bacteria that is used to control the caterpillar stage of plant-destroying moths and flies. It is a stomach poison that must be eaten by an insect in order to be toxic.

Baits: For consumer use, baits usually come in the form of gels, granules, or pastes that are enclosed in covered bait-tray containers. Baits typically use food grade material mixed with a poison.

Biodegradable: Almost all the products that are used for insect control will break down when exposed to the sun and the rain.

Boric acid: This slow-acting stomach poison attaches to insects more readily in its dry form. It is usually dispersed as a fine dust or in formulations for cockroach, ant and silverfish control. Roach-Prufe is a boric acid product.

Botanicals: This is the class of insecticides derived from plants. Examples include pyrethrum, rotenone, limonene and neem.

Brodifacoum: This single-dose anticoagulant rodenticide is formulated into various types of food baits and is effective against all species of rats and mice.

"Build Them Out": Using preventative structural measures, such as covering entry points with wire or mesh, to keep pests out of your house.

Cage Trap: A wire mesh trap that is constructed in such a way that when an animal enters the trap for a food bait, a trigger pan is touched and the door closes. Most cage traps are humane live traps.

Contact pesticides: These chemicals penetrate the body wall to cause death. Contact insecticides refer specifically to those chemicals that contact the outside of the insect's body directly during applications.

Desiccant insecticides: These products kill by removing or corroding the waxy outer coating on the insect's cuticle. This causes a loss of body fluids and the pest dies of dehydration. DE and Silica aerosol are two common examples.

Diatomaceous earth (DE): This powder is composed of the dried, calcified bodies of single-celled organisms called diatoms. Applied as a dust, DE is used to control cockroaches and other crawling insects by disrupting the waxy layers of the bug's cuticle, causing death by dehydration. DE is also very sharp and can cut the insects at their joints.

Dusts: These finely ground, dry formulations come in ready-to-use concentrations when purchased. Dusts are applied to surfaces or in cracks where insects run or hide, and are most effective when used in areas frequented by pests and nothing else. Moisture tends to make dusts less effective. After insects crawl over a dusted area, they inhale the poison or absorb it through their skin. Dusts are, in many cases, more effective than sprays. They are also not flammable and will usually not stain carpet and floors.

Emulsifiable concentrate (E.C.): A petroleum-based chemical is mixed with emulsifiers, thus enabling it to be mixed with water. When sprayed on a surface, a chemical residue is laid down that can't normally be seen.

Fipronil: A new insecticide that is used in very low dosages and works on the gama system of neurotransmitters of the insect.

Fogger: A pressurized can of insecticide that, when set off, will release fine particles of chemicals which remain airborne for a period of time.

Fumigants: These gaseous pesticides give off vapors that enter the pest's body through inhalation. Active ingredients are sometimes gasses that become liquids when packaged under pressure, and then become gasses again when released during application.

Glue boards: These sticky planks of cardboard are used either alone, or in traps. They snare pests who venture too close in search of food or some other type of bait and can be used for insects, rodents or snakes.

Granules: A pesticide that is mixed with a carrier, such as corn-cob. When water makes contact with the granules, the chemical is released in that area and the bugs are killed when they make contact with the treated surface.

Hydramethylnon: A slow-acting insecticide usually used in bait formulations, this chemical acts by disrupting energy metabolism within insect cells. It is most effective against cockroaches and colonies of ants.

Inorganic Insecticides: These are products that are normally mined from mineral deposits. Examples include boric acid, silica aerogel, and diatomaceous earth. They contain no carbon molecule.

Insect: Those creatures that have six legs, one or two pairs of wings, one pair of antennae and three body regions (head, thorax and abdomen). Their body is covered by a chitinous exoskeleton.

Insect Growth Regulators (IGRs): These chemicals mimic an insect's own juvenile hormone and disrupt normal growth and development. Variations include methoprene, and hydroprene. They are usually most successful when used against species with complete metamorphoses like fleas, roaches, mosquitoes and stored-product pests.

Metamorphosis: Refers to the changing in size and shape that an insect goes through from egg to adult. There are two types of metamorphoses: simple and complete.

Microencapsulated chemicals: These are formed when the insecticide particle is enclosed inside tiny spheres of nylon or some other polymer material. These particles readily pass through coarse screens and most sprayer nozzles. Note: this product has a long residual on the outside of your house.

Organophosphates: The primary toxic action of this class of insecticide involves inhibition of cholinesterase, an important enzyme in the nervous system. Disruption of these enzymes eventually causes muscle and organ failure, leading to the death of the insect.

Permethrin: A pyrethroid insecticide and tick repellent. It's used in a wide variety of ready-to-use or concentrated formulations to control many urban pests, but mainly for fleas and termites.

Pheromone: A substance produced by an insect to incite a response in other insects of the same species. Pheromones can also be created in a lab and are used in certain traps to attract target pests to their doom in glue.

Polymorphic: This means that the size of the colony will vary, from large individuals to small ones.

Pressurized liquid sprays: These products deposit a thin film of pesticide fogger directly on a target surface, rather than airborne droplets like most aerosol products. They work in the same manner as your typical pump-up type of sprayer.

Pyrethroids: These are synthetic versions of naturally occurring insecticides found in members of the chrysanthemum family.

Pyrethrin or pyrethrum: The active ingredients found in a species of chrysanthemum, these are available in a variety of concentrations and formulations. Because they are unstable chemically, these products are quick-acting, but have little residual effectiveness. Pyrethrum is frequently used to flush insects out of cracks and crevices. A contact kill product

Red fox urine: When used properly, the urine of a fox can help chase squirrels or raccoons out of attics. The pest animals believe that a predator is nearby and they leave very quickly.

Residual insecticide: This term usually refers to chemicals that leave a film-like layer—for a period of time—on treated surfaces where insects congregate or traverse.

Repellents: These are products that repel target pests by emitting a displeasing smell, unpleasant taste or predator odor.

RTU (Ready-to-Use) Sprays: These can be push-button aerosol cans or non-pressurized products that have a water base and are applied with a hand sprayer. The sprays are formed from a mixture of chemicals, stabilizers and water. Once sprayed on a surface, they will control bugs for 30 to 45 days in most cases.

Scats: The proper name for the droppings of mammals. If you know what made the droppings, you can identify the pest. The study of scats is called "Scatology."

Silica gel: This finely ground dust is composed of precipitated silicic acid and kills insects by desiccation through disruption of the waxy layer of the bug's body. Commercial formulations are usually combined with another insecticide—like pyrethrins—to reduce silica gel's tendency to diffuse from the treatment area. Silica gels are a fine dust and should not be inhaled.

Spray Solutions: A mixture of water or oil and one or more chemical substances. All of the ingredients dissolve to form a solution.

Stomach poisons: These pesticides must be swallowed to kill an insect or rodent. Most baits are examples of this formulation.

Warfarin: A multiple-dose anticoagulant rodenticide, warfarin is used as a dry powder with solid baits, but is also available for liquid baits. It may take several days worth of feedings to work, but is nonetheless effective on all species of rats and mice.

Weep Hole: Openings near the foundation of houses that are meant to facilitate ventilation. Normally found on the first layer of bricks around a foundation, weep holes occur every four or five bricks, where the cement in the mortar joint is left out.

Wettable Powders: These dry formulations are almost as fine-grained as dusts, however, they contain a higher degree of active ingredients. They must be mixed with water in order to be used. Care must be taken not to breathe the dust while mixing.

RESOURCES

Atlantic Paste and Glue (glue boards and traps) 800-458-7454
Bat Conservation International 512-327-9721
Beneficial Insectary 800-477-3715
Bio Quip Products (insect collecting material) 310-324-0620
Allen Special Products (copper mesh) 800-848-6805
Dr. T's Nature Products 800-299-6288
Eaton's Metal Tamper Resistant Rodent Stations 800-321-3421
Garden's Alive (organic garden supplier) 812-537-8650
Dirt Doctor's Dirt (Organic Newsletter) 817-485-6878
Live Beneficial Nematodes (Antidote) 800-524-1958
National Pesticide Network 800-858-7378
Natural Solutions (DE and other organic products) 888-231-9725
Nisus (Bora-Care and boric-based products) 800-264-0870
Ortho Products 800-225-2883
Ropel Animal and Bird Repellents 516-694-9000
Safer Soaps 800-654-1047
Specricide Products 800-332-5553
Tomahawk Live Traps (humane traps) 715-453-3550
Woodstream (rat and mouse snap traps) 800-800-1819

REQUEST FOR INSECT IDENTIFICATION
(Wanted Dead, Not Alive)

Professional pest control specialist Michael Bohdan will identify your insect specimen if you send a self-addressed, stamped envelope and a check for $10.00. In order to properly identify the specimen, it is necessary for you to send several specimens of the insect in a crush-proof container. Do not send specimens that have been squashed; do not put tape on specimens. This offer is good for home-infesting insects only—not plant bugs. Please send dead bugs only.

Complete this form and include it with your specimens.

Name: _____

Address: _____

State: _____ Zip Code: _____

Phone Number: _____

Date Collected, including year: _____

Location where found: _____

Any helpful information: _____

_____

Send your specimens, check, and SASE to:
    The Pest Shop, Inc.
    2231-B West 15th St.
    Plano, TX 75075
    Attn: Michael

BOOKS AVAILABLE FROM
SANTA MONICA PRESS

What's Buggin' You?
Michael Bohdan's Guide to
Home Pest Control
by Michael Bohdan
256 pages $12.95

Letter Writing Made Easy!
Volume 2
by Margaret McCarthy
224 pages $12.95

Offbeat Golf
A Swingin' Guide to a
Worldwide Obsession
by Bob Loeffelbein
192 pages $17.95

Heath Care Handbook
A Consumer's Guide to the
American Health Care System
by Mark Cromer
256 pages $12.95

The Book of Good Habits
Simple and Creative Ways to
Enrich Your Life
by Dirk Mathison
224 pages $9.95

Offbeat Museums
The Curators and Collections
of America's Most Unusual
Museums
by Saul Rubin
240 pages $17.95

Helpful Household Hints
by June King
224 pages $12.95

How to Win Lotteries,
Sweepstakes, and Contests
by Steve Ledoux
224 pages $12.95

Letter Writing Made Easy!
Featuring Sample Letters for
Hundreds of Common Occasions
by Margaret McCarthy
224 pages $12.95

How to Find Your Family Roots
The Complete Guide to Searching
for Your Ancestors
by William Latham
224 pages $12.95

ORDER FORM

1-800-784-9553

	Quantity	Amount
What's Buggin' You? ($12.95)	_____	_____
Letter Writing Made Easy! Volume 2 ($12.95)	_____	_____
Offbeat Golf ($17.95)	_____	_____
Health Care Handbook ($12.95)	_____	_____
The Book of Good Habits ($9.95)	_____	_____
Offbeat Museums ($17.95)	_____	_____
Helpful Household Hints ($12.95)	_____	_____
How to Win Lotteries, Sweepstakes... ($12.95)	_____	_____
Letter Writing Made Easy! ($12.95)	_____	_____
How to Find Your Family Roots ($12.95)	_____	_____

Subtotal _____

Shipping and Handling (see below) _____

CA residents add 8.25% sales tax _____

Total _____

Name _____

Address _____

City _____ State _____ Zip _____

Card Number _____ Exp _____

☐ Visa   ☐ MasterCard

Signature _____

☐ Enclosed is my check or money order payable to:

Santa Monica Press LLC
P.O. Box 1076
Dept. 1019
Santa Monica, CA 90406

1-800-784-9553

Shipping and Handling	
1 book	$3.00
2–3 books	$4.00
Each additional book is	$ .50